Praise for *Power through Partnership*

"Having been a part of a founding trio of women for nearly a decade now, I am often amazed when people express surprise that such a partnership exists—and has thrived for so many years. I'm gratified to see Betsy Polk and Maggie Ellis Chotas focus specifically on partnerships between women and explore their unique attributes and strengths. Shining a light on successful partnerships can only encourage more of such partnerships!"
—**Elisa Camahort Page, cofounder and COO, BlogHer, Inc.**

"This is the book for every woman eager for a better way to work and lead. Through partnership, women are capitalizing on strengths and leveraging dynamic networks of sisters, friends, and colleagues to achieve success. *Power through Partnership* shows the way!"
—**Joanna Strober, coauthor of *Getting to 50/50* and CEO, Kurbo Health**

"Need more flexibility in your life? More support? More inspiration? The solution is simple: find a business partner! Polk and Chotas have written a thoughtful and practical guide to forming and sustaining a partnership. As someone with a longtime writing partner (my brother!), I found myself nodding a lot as I read."
—**Dan Heath, coauthor of the *New York Times* bestsellers *Made to Stick*, *Switch*, and *Decisive***

"Business rhetoric is full of heroic soloists—but the deeper truth is that no business succeeds alone. The great success stories derive speed, spread, and impact from partnerships and alliances. This book is a critical contribution to the business story of the century: the rise of female entrepreneurship."
—**Margaret Heffernan, author of *Willful Blindness* and *A Bigger Prize***

"In the midst of the heated debate between the stay-at-homes and the frantic-jugglers, the resentful who had to stop and the resentful who wish they could, *Power through Partnership* shines a light on an exciting option for women everywhere. In this thoughtful and thorough examination of the benefits of partnership, Betsy Polk and Maggie Ellis Chotas provide us with a blueprint for leveraging what women do best: working together."
—**Emma McLaughlin and Nicola Kraus, coauthors of *The Nanny Diaries* and business partners for thirteen years**

Power Through Partnership

POWER
THROUGH
PARTNERSHIP

HOW WOMEN
LEAD BETTER
TOGETHER

BETSY POLK AND MAGGIE ELLIS CHOTAS

BK™

Berrett–Koehler Publishers, Inc.
San Francisco
a BK Business book

Berrett-Koehler Publishers, Inc.
1333 Broadway, Suite 1000
Oakland, CA 94612-1921
Tel: (510) 817-2277   Fax: (510) 817-2278   www.bkconnection.com

Ordering Information
Quantity sales. Special discounts are available on quantity purchases by corporations, associations, and others. For details, contact the "Special Sales Department" at the Berrett-Koehler address above.

Individual sales. Berrett-Koehler publications are available through most bookstores. They can also be ordered directly from Berrett-Koehler: Tel: (800) 929-2929; Fax: (802) 864-7626; www.bkconnection.com

Orders for college textbook/course adoption use. Please contact Berrett-Koehler:
Tel: (800) 929-2929; Fax: (802) 864-7626.

Orders by U.S. trade bookstores and wholesalers. Please contact Ingram Publisher Services,
Tel: (800) 509-4887; Fax: (800) 838-1149; E-mail: customer.service@ingrampublisherservices.com; or visit www.ingrampublisherservices.com/Ordering for details about electronic ordering.

Berrett-Koehler and the BK logo are registered trademarks of Berrett-Koehler Publishers, Inc.

Printed in the United States of America

Berrett-Koehler books are printed on long-lasting acid-free paper. When it is available, we choose paper that has been manufactured by environmentally responsible processes. These may include using trees grown in sustainable forests, incorporating recycled paper, minimizing chlorine in bleaching, or recycling the energy produced at the paper mill.

Library of Congress Cataloging-in-Publication Data
Polk, Betsy.
Power through partnership : how women lead better together / Betsy Polk
and Maggie Ellis Chotas. — First edition.
    pages cm
Summary: "Female partnerships are deeply rewarding and a powerful way
for women to advance in a world still suffering from gender bias. So why
don't women work together more often? Polk and Chotas address the myths
and fears that keep women from partnering and offer expert advice on how
to make female partnerships thrive"— Provided by publisher.
ISBN 978-1-62656-158-8 (paperback)
1. Women executives. 2. Women professional employees. 3. Partnership.
4. Leadership in women. I. Title.
HD6054.3.P65 2014
658.4'092082--dc23
                        2014023983

First Edition
19 18 17 16 15   14   10 9 8 7 6 5 4 3 2

Cover Designer: Irene Morris
Book Producer and Designer: Detta Penna
Copyeditor: Sandra Craig
Indexer: Rachel Rice

With love and immense gratitude to our families—
Marc, Michael, and Annie Joseph
and
Harrell, Georgia, and Nicholas Chotas.
And to all the partners who so generously shared their stories.

Contents

Foreword

I love this book. Really. And not just because Betsy Polk and Maggie Ellis Chotas say nice things about my article, "Why Women Still Can't Have It All." But because they offer real, practical solutions to the dilemmas that face even the most ambitious and committed women among us. Indeed, our ambition and commitment both to what we do and the people we love are precisely what create so many competing demands on our time. In that context, many of us deflect or defer leadership positions at the top of big organizations, worrying that taking on responsibilities and duties to hundreds and thousands of people will tip the balance of our lives irrevocably and irremediably.

That is where partnership comes in. Listen to how Betsy and Maggie describe their own work. Looking around a café one morning at both stay-at-home moms and career women heading off to their daily commute, they reflected, "Our lives—filled with spouses, children and activity—were sane. We were leading the way we wanted to, on our own clocks, in cafes, at client sites, in our home offices, and even on trails, where we took long 'strategy talk' walks together. Thanks to our work together, as two women who each understood where the other was coming from, we were happy."

That is a vision that women (and men) should relate and aspire to. Why shouldn't we "lead the way we want to," making time for all the different parts of our lives and ourselves in ways that make us happier, healthier, and more productive? The trick, they say, is to find a partner, not only someone you can share burdens with and create the flexibility you so badly need, but also someone who will motivate you and hold you accountable.

I think the reason this book resonates so powerfully with me is that it taps the secret of much of my own success, certainly as a scholar. Early on, I found that if I took on a project with a co-author, I would not let that person down. I might have let *myself* down, deciding that obligations to committee work, teaching, or family were more important than scholarship. But I would never let down another person to whom I had made a commitment. So finding a partner was actually a way of making sure I did the things I knew I should really do for myself.

Partnership can be an important path to power for women. Read this book and take the plunge. You will be re-inventing the work world and opening up to creating a whole new vista of opportunity for yourself along the way.

Anne-Marie Slaughter
President and CEO, New America
Author of "Why Women Still Can't Have It All,"
The Atlantic, June/July 2012.

Out from Under the Radar

Quick. Who comes to mind when you think of male partnerships? We asked ourselves that question and came up with an impressive list of men who have made a sizable impact on the world: hugely successful ice cream entrepreneurs Ben and Jerry; historically revered explorers Lewis and Clark; cultural icons and famed magicians Penn and Teller; mega-hit film producers Bob and Harvey Weinstein; Google co-founders Larry Page and Sergey Brin; DNA discoverers Watson and Crick; *Book of Mormon* and *Southpark* creators Matt Stone and Trey Parker, to name just a few.

Now think of female partners. How many can you cite? If you're drawing a blank, you're not alone. Yes, there are plenty of powerful female partners out there—we know that is true after interviewing 125 of them—but none have immediate recognition like the men on the list above.

Figuring we were overlooking the obvious, we turned to Google. Here's who popped up: Lucy and Ethel, the zany duo of 1950s television fame, two best friends who were always scheming (often unsuccessfully, though hilariously) to out-wit their husbands; Laverne and Shirley, the Milwaukee beer bottlers, roommates, and sitcom characters who struggled to make it in life and love; Cagney and Lacey, two smart, tough television cops; and Thelma and Louise, movie heroines who, when all roads led to despair, drove their car off a cliff.

When it comes to men working together as partners, there are plenty of accessible, successful, top-of-mind role models. Also, the men on that list are not only well known as individuals, they are recognized as intentional partners as well—that is, men who deliberately decided to work together. What's more, all are or were living, breathing people who have accomplished great things together. And, on the whole, they are recognized more for the successes they've achieved than for their friendships or any interfering personality conflicts.

And that list of women partners? For starters, not one of them is or was a real person—they all lived on television and movie screens—and they are all long gone. Thelma and Louise, the most recent of the batch, had their heyday in 1991. That list of men is loaded with co-leaders who are scientists, technology innovators, entrepreneurs, creative collaborators, and entertainers, but their female counterparts are in an imaginary world. We could not find any professional women part-ners in visible, intentional collaborations in our online search of cultural icons. And even in the fantasy world, none of the women were known as business partners and certainly not as co-leaders. They were friends, yes, with personality conflicts and mishaps that often took center stage—but partners? Unless you count Cagney and Lacey, far from it. What's wrong with this picture?

The Takeaway

The easy answer is that partnership is a way of working that suits men but not women. However, that's only half the truth. Yes, there's plenty of evidence that partnership works for men. But what we've learned from our research and interviews with female co-leaders in a range of fields is that it definitely works for women as well. From our interviewees—who are collaborating as investment bankers, singer-songwriters, peace mediators, script writers, wholesalers, gallery owners, cupcake bakers, newspaper publishers, and social media whizzes—we heard the same message over and over: partnership is a professional model with the power to make life work more successful and life itself a whole lot saner for women who are ready for a better way.

Maybe that's you. Perhaps you are reading *Power Through Partnership* because you are ready for new solutions to old problems, are tired of working at full tilt, weary from striving for perfection. With partnership the hard work is still there, of course, but it is accompanied by the steady support of a female colleague who is equally committed to pursuing a vision you share, one that's based on values you both hold. Sound like a pipe dream? It's not when partners are ready, willing, and able to do the communicating, load sharing, and relationship building it takes to create and sustain healthy collaborations.

How Do We Know?

As the co-leaders of The Mulberry Partners, the consulting practice we founded in 2002 that combines our complementary backgrounds in education and organization development, we directly experience the reality that partnership can create. So do the female co-leaders we've interviewed, who are benefitting from the flexibility and support it provides, the confidence it builds, the mutual accountability it encourages, and the equity that is available through it.

The Book We Couldn't Find

With benefits like these, you'd think that female dynamic duos would be an entrepreneurial norm. That's what we thought too when we decided to join forces. We knew we wanted to partner, but we had questions about what it would mean for our decades-long preexisting friendship. We began our partnership aware and wary of the conflict that can brew between women and hinder collaboration. Early in her career, Betsy witnessed the implosions of two sets of female collaborations. In both cases, communication was the first casualty. Partners too busy doing the work to check in with each other made assumptions, trust evaporated quickly, and poorly managed conflict followed. The results were fractured projects, broken businesses, and, what seemed to be most painful of all, damaged relationships. These were scenarios we wanted to avoid, but how? What steps could we take to build a strong, vibrant partnership?

Introduction: Out from Under the Radar

Eager for guidance about how to develop a successful partnership with a healthy relationship at the center, we looked everywhere for relevant advice. We found many books and resources about how to set up partnership agreements, others on the joys of friendship, and still others on the ups and downs faced by female entrepreneurs. But nowhere did we find a guide that spoke to us as women who wanted to combine our professional skills to create a successful entity while making sure we preserved our personal relationship.

In retrospect it's not surprising that we couldn't find resources about professional women's partnerships. Why would these guides exist when this model is barely recognized in the larger culture? Unlike the celebrated list of male collaborators, who inspire new collaborations by serving as visible role models, real-life successful female collaborations are a well-kept secret—unknown and unaddressed.

With only our own experiences and awareness of potential pitfalls and conflicts to guide us, we set out to form a partnership that could work effectively and be personally fulfilling. And after twelve years of co-leadership, we deem our partnership an unqualified success. The benefits have been enormous. Our partnership has consistently worked for us, providing a platform for professional success through a relationship that offers the flexibility, support, and confidence that energizes us. Because of our partnership, we've been able to give each other steady support as we've faced obstacles. We've felt the rare freedom of being our whole selves at work, knowing that we both fully appreciate our strengths and our quirks. We've fueled each other's confidence as we've encouraged each other to take on new challenges. We've had the flexibility of scheduling client meetings and other commitments around our children's school schedules.

We began wondering if we were unusually fortunate or if other women were achieving similar benefits from their collaborations. If so, could partnership be a replicable model more women would benefit from? We decided to find out.

Detective Work: Finding Women Partners

To obtain answers to these questions, we first had to find other women partners. This was no easy task. (You already know what happened when we turned to Google for help with this quest.) We had to hone our detective skills, zeroing in on such clues as "co-founder" and "co-president" in articles about women in leadership. Not once did we discover a female partnership announcing themselves as such.

It took nearly a decade to assemble our list, but eventually we interviewed 125 female co-leaders, who, once found, had plenty to say about the power of their partnerships. Our interviews morphed into long conversations, as women enthusiastically shared their stories. Many confided that they are rarely asked about their collaborations, yet they revealed that these collaborations are often what make their success possible.

These conversations confirmed that partnership is a workable leadership model for women with varying experience in many fields. Whether partners had known each other for a lifetime or hadn't laid eyes on each other until someone else matched them up, our interviewees validated our positive experiences. It was more than just our good fortune. It was a broader phenomenon bringing the enormous benefits of success, satisfaction, and even happiness to many women's lives. The results of our interviews led us to believe that partnership is a model that indeed could be replicable for many additional women.

Needed: New Options

Goodness knows women need better professional options. Experts such as Stephanie Coontz have concluded that the "gender revolution has not hit a stall, it's hit a wall,"[1] and numerous statistics and studies confirm that women's rise toward equity in the workplace has halted. In 2012, Anne-Marie Slaughter's groundbreaking *Atlantic* article, "Why Women Still Can't Have It All," dispelled the myths that all women really need to do to succeed is to work harder and stay on the career ladder. Arguing that it isn't women who are not succeeding, it's the system that's failing women, Slaughter writes, "I still strongly believe that women can 'have it all' (and that men can too). I believe that we can 'have it all at the same time.' But not today, not with the way America's economy and society are currently structured."[2]

After impressive gains in education parity and a wider presence in a range of once-male-dominated fields, women seem to have gone as far as they can go as leaders until changes are made to this structure, the very fabric of our culture. Entrenched social, cultural, and governmental structural impediments are holding women back. Disparities in health care; gaps in equal pay; limited (and unpaid) family leave; lack of affordable, high-quality options for child and elder care—to name only a few—push back against women at all levels of work. And while there are individual exceptions, such as the twenty-six female CEOs of the top 500 companies[3] and the 3.3 percent of corporate board chairs who are female,[4] too many barriers still work against women in general to prevent them from making it into top leadership in large numbers.

Take the portrait Frank Bruni painted of his hardworking, multitasking sister in his *New York Times* column "Women's Unequal Lot." A look at her life compared to his leaves Bruni stunned. He has one job; she has three or four. In addition to her paid work in an executive recruiting firm, she spends "many hours daily as a combined chauffeur, drill sergeant, cheerleader and emotional nursemaid for her two children and two stepchildren." And she serves on her local board of education. Oh yeah, and she's hosting Easter dinner for the whole extended family. We couldn't help but think of our sisters, mothers, and friends, nodding with recognition as Bruni summed up the reality, "Being at the helm would probably push my sister over the edge."[5]

Frank Bruni's sister, like countless other women, needs new options and real solutions. That's where partnership comes in. It is an option and real solution that men have long been leveraging. Look at the successful models listed at the beginning of this book. These men have tapped into the power that grows from partnership. They've made the most of the extra strength that results from the transition from one leader to multiple leaders, who can create a more forceful presence. We keep thinking about a picture we saw of the all-male Twitter co-founders who were standing together on the floor of the New York Stock Exchange after Twitter's initial public offering. There they stood amidst the chaos, the epitome of success—confident, assured, and powerful. They took up space. Their declaration seemed to be *We are here, we are important, and we are making an impact.*[6]

The same needs to be true for women. Although female partners are not now as visible (something we're here to change), they do have an impact in their respective fields and greater equity because of their collective force.

Not a One-Size-Fits-All Solution

We know that partnership is not for everyone. Sharing leadership doesn't always work, even with the right partner, the right timing, and all the benefits. And many women are successful and content working alone, preferring to lead on their own. Some women may prefer not to invest in the levels of commitment and relationship maintenance required to make partnership work. We know we cannot change that, nor do we want to. But we do see that this model of female partnership applies to intentional, ongoing collaborations as well as to situational, short-term opportunities to lead together. Whatever the extent of the collaboration—from co-leading a business to spearheading a short-term project—it will be enhanced when women enter the situation with myths debunked, eyes wide open, and with communication and conflict-resolution skills at the ready.

The Next Step

Once upon a time we took our friendship and started a business without any idea about what we were getting into. When we didn't find the resources we needed, we reached out and found 125 female partner mentors and role models to guide, inspire, and encourage us to keep at it. Through the example of these trail-blazing women, we have been assured that the benefits of partnership are strong, palpable, and well within reach, and that the challenges are conquerable because we have each other. These partners who have shared so generously of their time and wisdom are the ones to replace the outdated, make-believe partners of old.

After all, who needs Lucy and Ethel when Heather White and Lori Joyce are leading bakeries in Canada and starring in their own reality show, *The Cupcake Girls*? Who needs Cagney and Lacey when Marcia Greenberger and Nancy Duff Campbell of the National Women's Law Center are setting policies that combat the structural impediments that work against women? And who needs Thelma and Louise when Valerie Batts and Angela Bryant, co-founders of VISIONS,

Inc., are teaching CEOs across the globe how to dismantle gender biases and racism in order to gain true equity?

We wrote *Power Through Partnership* for women because, quite simply, no other resources available now carry this message for women. Sure, plenty of valuable sources make the case that life is tough—exhorting women to "lean in," to stop trying to be Wonder Woman, or to let go of being overwhelmed. But how are women supposed to do that? Concrete ideas and solutions are needed. Partnership is a practical professional model that works well for too many women to be buried. Men have been partnering for a long time, guided by lists of accessible models for help and inspiration. It's time for the same assistance to be available to women.

It's our mission to place the model of women's partnership front and center as a practical, accessible, effective solution. This book is for women who are ready for a better way to lead, to work, to live. Is that you? It has certainly been us. This is the guidebook we never had, here to help you navigate as you experience the benefits, face down the obstacles, debunk the myths, and strengthen the communication and conflict tools you're going to need for the rich and winding partnership road ahead.

Why Partnership Works for Women

The story behind our trust in the power of partnership begins with two frizzy-haired high school sophomores who met in English class and united over a class project, a *Saturday Night Live* take on Ray Bradbury's *The Martian Chronicles*, set to the music of the B-52s. We received an A. The external validation was nice, but best of all, we had a lot of fun bouncing ideas off each other, writing and rewriting, and spending hours thinking creatively together. After high school, we promised ourselves that someday we'd work together for real.

We held on to the idea of partnering even while our professional lives took different paths—Betsy as a consultant working with a range of institutions to bolster communication and collaboration, and Maggie as a teacher and school administrator. In 2002, when we found ourselves living in the same North Carolina area code, experiencing similar career transitions and with three young children between us, we started getting serious. What would it look like for us to lead together? How could we combine Betsy's background in organization development consulting with Maggie's experience in education? Marathon phone calls and long talks while pushing kids in strollers resulted in The Mulberry Partners, our education-focused practice for organization development, coaching, and consulting.

We were not surprised to realize, early on, that this entrepreneurial partnership suited us. Having a business, an actual entity, made us accountable to each other in ways we would have found difficult to justify otherwise. Back then, as the mothers of young children, we found it difficult to carve out time for ourselves without feeling guilty. But scheduling time together for a professional endeavour elevated this time from me-time to sanctioned time focused on reaching goals. Through this sense of shared responsibility grew a credibility that fueled our confidence, which enhanced our business, attracting clients and leading to growth.

A few years after we founded Mulberry, in the middle of our weekly meeting, huddled over laptops at one of our favorite coffee shops, it suddenly struck us that we were happy with our work, our leadership, and our lives. We were doing what by then was second nature—building on ideas, communicating in our partnership shorthand, respecting each other's expertise, and trusting that the outcomes of our meeting would reflect a united front.

We surveyed the crowd of mostly women surrounding us in the café, comparing our lot with theirs. A lively group of moms seemed as busy as we were, but their focus was distracted as they tried to converse while keeping small children entertained. Lined up at the coffee bar were some business-suited women handling calls while ordering espresso for their morning commutes.

Were these women as satisfied as we were? We hoped so. But as coaches who work with a wide range of people, we were beginning to see that ours was a rare reality. So many of the women we knew—whether they were solo entrepreneurs, corporate employees, or stay-at-home moms—were struggling to opt out, opt back in, or just stay afloat. They were often plagued by doubt and insecurity as they strived for something more.

And there we were, marching to our own beat, with someone by our side who had as much skin in the game. We had expanded a twenty-year friendship into a business that helped schools, nonprofit organizations, and corporations to develop collaborative cultures. We were bringing forth the best of ourselves without second-guessing the value of our contribution. We were engaged in work we enjoyed, reaching goals based on our own values that we were equally and fully vested in. We trusted ourselves and each other to fulfill a shared vision. Our work was successful. Our lives—filled with spouses, children, and activity—were sane. We were leading the way we wanted to, on our own clocks, in cafés, at client sites, in our home offices, and even on trails, where we held long "strategy talks" as we walked. Thanks to our work together, we were two women who understood where the other was coming from, and we were happy.

Overload: A Female Conundrum

Consider the women you know. How many are struggling to squeeze even more into already packed lives? How many are saying yes too often and no all too rarely? How many are trying to convince themselves that perfection is just beyond the horizon, that all they have to do is work harder, sleep less, push more, smile wider, be tougher, and maybe they will get there, somehow, someday. These women—we've certainly been among them—are striving to be superwomen, summoning all their energy to reach a mirage of perfection, trying to scale mountains of exalted expectations (their own and those of others) as they struggle to lean in deeper and deeper.

When we suggest partnership as a practical solution to these women, their eyes light up as they imagine this professional relationship with someone who is just as focused on achieving similar goals and is equally committed to sharing responsibilities. But then a shadow of doubt crosses their faces as they remind themselves of all the reasons partnership just can't work. Their explanations run the gamut: the fear of trusting someone else; anxiety about conflict; and worry about not having enough time, smarts, skills, money, and/or talent to contribute to a fifty-fifty collaboration. Perhaps they can see the ultimate value of partnership, but the time and energy the investment requires and the penalty if it doesn't work out seem to make the risks too huge to take the chance.

But what if these undecided women could see many high-visibility female role models demonstrating that through collaboration they are leading more capably without running themselves ragged? Perhaps then they could see that those advantages of partnering that seemed too good to be true are indeed real and well within reach.

What if women saw the possibility of partnership as a logical, radical way of working? It is logical because collaboration makes sense, builds on strengths, and provides a way for women to operate in a world that continues to be gender inequitable. And it is radical because as much sense as partnership makes for women, especially now, as women struggle to succeed in this inequitable world, the path to partnership has been obscured by myths, misconceptions, and negative messages, turning what should be a logical decision to team up with an ally into an off-the-beaten-path alternative.

Until now, anyway. Instead of partnership remaining a glimmer in the eye of an overworked superwoman that is too easily wiped away as an impossible dream, we want it to be an accessible, equitable choice for women as they make decisions about their work lives.

The Benefits of Partnership

We want to change the world, transforming the ways in which women work by spreading the message about the tremendous benefits that can be realized in healthy female partnerships, such as flexibility, confidence, freedom, support, mutual accountability—and happiness.

Flexibility

Flexibility is a major partnership asset that provides the space and trust for one partner to step forward as the other leans back. Then, with barely a flutter, there's room for the roles to shift. Whether it's balancing a job share, adjusting dynamics in a client meeting, or filling in for each other when a sick child is at home, women in partnership know how to step up or step back depending on what is needed in the moment.

Kirsten "Kiwi" Smith, half of the screenwriting duo behind such blockbuster movies as *Legally Blonde,* shared a story that demonstrates this partnership balancing act. Kiwi and partner Karen McCullah Lutz were pitching their script for a movie for the sixth time to Hollywood executives, and things were not going well. As Kiwi tells it, "I kept pushing Karen to do these meetings and she didn't want to anymore, so this time it was up to me. I pitched my heart out, and the producer said it was the worst thing he'd ever heard. While I was lying on the floor practically crying, Karen picked up the pitch and kept it going. It's a good thing she did. They said yes." The result of Kiwi and Karen's flexible persistence was the movie *The Ugly Truth*.

But imagine that it was just Kiwi in the story. She might still have been on the floor crying while the executives stepped over her to go for lunch. If it was just Karen, she would have given up the pitch after the third try. Later in our interview, Kiwi remarked, "The male screenwriters I've worked with tend to just focus on getting the job done. For women, the relationship lines tend to zigzag between personal and professional, and back again." It's those zigzagging lines that make women's collaborations more than just business arrangements, giving them texture, complexity, and meaning.

Unfortunately, the lines of the traditional work world often don't allow the same sort of zigzagging. Most workplaces are set up around the idea of the ideal worker: someone who is available to give his heart, soul, and life to the company. As Brigid Schulte describes in her bestseller *Overwhelmed: Love, Work, and Play When No One Has the Time:*

> The ideal worker doesn't take parental leave when a child is born. He doesn't need a place or time to pump breast milk. He has no need of family-friendly policies like flexible scheduling, part-time work, or telecommuting. The ideal worker doesn't have to find babysitters, deal with school closures on snow days, or otherwise worry about child-care responsibilities.... The ideal worker never has to think about researching good assisted-care facilities for Mom or Dad as they get older, whether they're getting the best treatment in ICU, or how to get his sister to her next chemotherapy appointment. It's simply not his job.[7]

Schulte concludes that the ideal worker is "so tied to his job that he works endless hours, even if it costs him his health and his family." Though this is a bit exaggerated, there are plenty of work environments where this stranglehold is the reality. A mere mention of the idea of flexibility in one of these places could cause you to be treated as if you were yelling out a bomb threat, and you could be whisked away into a secure location. Sounds far-fetched, right? Sadly, it's not. While in graduate school, Maggie interviewed for a job. She was in the middle of an office tour when the woman who was interviewing her began describing the benefits of the position. "What about the four-day-a-week option we discussed earlier?" Maggie asked. The interviewer glanced furtively at the cubicles surrounding them and whispered, "This isn't something to be talked about out here." Maggie was quickly escorted into a private office to discuss what turned out to be a hush-hush topic.

Often flexibility is brought up in relationship to child-rearing, but interviews with partners show that isn't just parents who want or need it. When the father of Summer Bricknell of LocoPops Gourmet Popsicles, a chain of Mexican-style popsicles, was bedridden, Summer was able to be with him and support her mother, thanks to her partnership with Connie Semans. As Summer told us, "Without a partner, it would be much harder for me to take time away from the business. Loco-Pops would go by the wayside and I would be on to the next big thing." Instead, she was able to take time away, knowing the business would be in good hands with Connie at the helm.

While flexibility is a benefit of any type of partnership, regardless of gender, the reality is that women still do the majority of the caregiving in families, from child to elder care. According to the National Alliance for Caregiving and AARP, an estimated 66 percent of informal caregivers are female.[8] Without flexible work options, women typically end up spending twelve more years out of the workforce compared with men.[9] The truth is that women need the kind of flexibility partnership can provide in order to stay engaged in the workforce for the long haul. This doesn't necessarily mean they will work less, but it often means that they will adapt and do what's needed to get it all done, achieving results on multiple fronts.

Cali Ressler and Jody Thompson share a passion for promoting the kinds of results-oriented workplaces that engage today's leaders—both women and men. What started at Best Buy as an innovative human resources project became ROWE, Results-Only Work Environment, the independent company Cali and Jody founded to focus on helping workplaces such as the White House become focused on results. Who better than two women partners to make the case for how the way flexibility can transform the world of work?

Confidence

We can say from our perspective as coaches that no matter how smart, how together, how polished a woman might seem, chances are that some seeds of self-doubt lurk right below the surface. This theory was reinforced when we started working with a coaching client who struck us as the epitome of competence in her role as head of a successful independent school. When she called for our help, we were delighted by the opportunity to work with such an esteemed, beloved leader. Yet when we met with her, the strong exterior was quickly cast aside, revealing a muddle of misgivings about decisions she had made and communications she had delivered.

Most people, women as well as men, face moments when they question and critique the person in the mirror, but what surprised us in this case and in so many others is how little it takes for a woman, compared with a man, to doubt her abilities. Of course, men suffer from their fair share of moments of doubt. But for women, who are operating on inequitable playing fields and often under immense expectations for perfection in all aspects of complex lives, normal human feelings of insecurity can turn into suffocating self-doubts. This way of thinking is so prevalent for women that in 1978, Pauline Clance and Suzanne Imes identified the "imposter syndrome"[10] to describe the sense of phoniness successful women can feel when they achieve.

Although the imposter syndrome was first studied in the 1970s, the nagging effect of lack of confidence in high-achieving women continues to be a hot topic today. In *The Confidence Code: The Science and Art of Self-Assurance: What Women Should Know*, Katty Kay and Claire Shipman explain, "For years, women have kept our heads down and played by the rules. We have made undeniable progress. Yet we still haven't reached the heights we know we are capable of scaling."[11] This lack of confidence has a profound effect on many women's sense of self and feelings of efficacy. Without the confidence to ask for what they want and sureness in their ideas, according to Shipman and Kay, it's rare for women to get into the upper echelons of leadership. And the few women who do reach that level often doubt that they deserve to be there.

The partnership dynamic plays a powerful role in developing confidence. The process starts with deciding to partner. When you say yes to combining your skills with those of a respected peer, you need to first acknowledge that you're bringing valuable skills and perspectives to the partnership: after all, your partner is choosing you for good reasons. And, while you may sometimes experience the imposter syndrome yourself, chances are you have faith in the credibility of your partner: a woman may cut herself down, but rarely will she transfer that insecurity to her close colleague. Through the very act of partnering, women learn to assume confidence in themselves because their professional identity is closely tied to that of their partner's.

As we were writing this book, we considered the influence of our own partnership and realized we had both experienced a boost in self-esteem from sharing each other's confidence. Whenever we've faced a task that seemed challenging, all we had to do was remind ourselves that together we were sure to figure it out. Knowing that we could count on drawing from a deeper well of confidence turned what could have been anxiety into we-can-do-it enthusiasm and success.

Freedom

We live in a world where "brusque" is code for another *B*-word used to describe a woman in leadership whose power intimidates others, whereas for men such assertive behavior is a perk of leadership and is often expected. Similarly, although showing emotion is often considered a feminine weakness, it can be perceived as a male strength. Jon Stewart deftly handled this gender double standard in a segment of *The Daily Show* entitled "The Broads Must Be Crazy." Stewart juxtaposed a picture of a misty-eyed Hillary Clinton with photos of male politicians breaking down in tears. Whereas the media's response to Clinton included comments deriding her for "letting her emotions fall out of her" and "having mood swings," the teary-eyed males received praise from reporters for being "passionate" and "honest." The comparisons led Stewart to proclaim, with his typical acerbic wit, "It's OK to be a pussy, as long as you have a dick."[12]

In sharp contrast to the entrenched double standards that plague our society, women in partnership have access to the freedom that comes from working with someone who gets it because she has been operating on the same playing field, under the same unspoken rules and societal expectations. This shared understanding can make it easier for a woman to bring her entire self to work, knowing that in the company of a female peer there's no need to modify, adjust, or apologize for who she really is. Partnership is one of the few professional spheres (perhaps the only one) in which women can comfortably be themselves—brusque, emotional, or otherwise—in contrast to more structured, mixed-gender environments, where women might not feel so at ease.

Kendall Allen, who, with Elizabeth Bleser, led a business unit for Incognito Digital, an online marketing firm, described her appreciation of this freedom, "It's really, really nice to have a female partner to discuss male-female dynamics that are sometimes power, sometimes sexual. It's nice to have a partner who gets it—it's a surprise benefit of working with a woman."

Through their collaboration, Kendall and Elizabeth also found the freedom to stretch beyond their usual personal and professional comfort zones. According to Kendall, "Through this collaboration, I've been able to explore boundaries that I know I could never explore with a male partner—this is both a personal benefit and a professional one." Elizabeth added, "In my partnership with Kendall, I feel completely comfortable telling her when I don't feel confident or comfortable. If she were male I wouldn't feel as comfortable."

Steady Support

Much of what makes this freedom possible is the support partners give each other, in a fluid give-and-take way. Support, the secret sauce of partnership, is often difficult to ask for. T his can be especially true for women, who may feel that by needing to ask for help, they are falling short of the giant expectations they've set for themselves. But the beauty of partnership is that reciprocal support must exist for the partnership to work. Partners know that to achieve their goals, they must be there for each other, each of them giving and receiving support. Think back to Kiwi and Karen's story. If Kiwi hadn't accepted Karen's supportive step-in, she would have defeated the outcomes they were trying to achieve together. This balanced support isn't just nice to have—it's an essential component of an effective collaboration that enables women working at full tilt to reach goals in ways that invigorate instead of depleting them.

According to Linda Kaplan Thaler, the mutual support she shared with co-founder and co-author Robin Koval was key to their success. Linda and Robin, the former co-leaders of Kaplan Thaler, one of the fastest-growing advertising agencies in the United States and the creative force behind such iconic advertising campaigns as the Aflac duck, have also written several books together. Linda shared with us her strategy for ensuring the support required of this fifteen-year collaboration, "To make it work, always put your partner's needs ahead of yours. If you're both looking out for each other, it works out. It's more than just watching each other's backs," she continued. "It's extreme empathy—it is literally seeing it from her point of view." The emphasis on empathy is woven into the values of Kaplan Thaler, where people are as important as any outcomes produced, and it was the key message in Linda and Robin's first book, *The Power of Nice*.

Robin put a different spin on the value of support to leaders, "It can be very lonely and scary to be making these decisions on your own. You always have colleagues, but being at the top puts you in a position where you can be quite lonely. Having a partner provides a great sense of security and counsel, and a way to bounce off your ideas that you just don't have in a single leadership position. It is hard to lead from a position of solitude. As human beings, we don't work that well that way, yet the workplace has evolved leadership into solitary silos."

Women certainly can and do lead and "lean in" alone with great success, but with the give-and-take support of working with the right partner, they can discover that working together and leading as equals can be a more effective and satisfying way of accomplishing their goals. They can learn that partnership, in which each partner is there for the other, is in the best interests of their product or service. No longer need women strive alone in solitary silos. Women in partnership are making big decisions and taking action together. Rather than lonely, the top is an exciting, energizing, supportive place to be!

Mutual Accountability

When you have the confidence to trust your partner's intentions, knowing you can count on her as she counts on you, chances are you're going to do all you can to deliver. Stephanie Allen, co-founder with Tina Kuna of Dream Dinners, a nationally franchised meal-preparation company, likens this benefit to having a workout buddy who keeps you walking around the track. As Stephanie said, "You might not go out for a run when it is rainy and cold because it's just too much trouble. But if you know your friend is waiting for you on the corner, you're not going to leave her standing out in the rain alone waiting for you to show up. So you go for your run, and you're glad you did, but it's not because of you—even though you know it's good for you and you should. You do it because you don't want to let your friend down."

Partnership is the same. Knowing someone else is counting on you gives women the push that can be needed to move past the imposter syndrome so results can be achieved. Partners can't give up on their dreams because these dreams are fueling the outcomes of their partnership, and each partner is accountable to the other for seeing it through. On the flip side, when we asked female partners to describe what motivated their partnerships, they often cited the fear of letting their partner down as the inspiration that kept them going. Mutual accountability is a big expectation, but it can be an energizing one when it comes from partners who are invested in achieving the same results.

Happiness

Of all the enormous, life-altering advantages of partnership, the one that consistently rose to the top in conversations with partners was, quite simply, the happiness that comes when the relationship at the core satisfies all partners. As Gretchen Rubin writes in *The Happiness Project,* women gain joy when they find a close connection and intimacy in relationship, and these are natural outcomes of the rich relationship at the heart of women's healthy collaborations. As Stephanie Wilkinson, cofounder of *Brain, Child: The Magazine for Thinking Mothers,* put it, "For this partnership to work is one of the most gratifying things in life."

Chapter 1: Why Partnership Works for Women

We've found in our interviews that it's the relationship at the center of women's collaborations that makes them tick. When the connection between partners is healthy, the overall entity will be healthy; and when the relationship is suffering, results often suffer as well. Generally speaking, the same is not true for male partners, who tend to measure success by revenue and results.

Women don't have to be best friends or even friends to become partners. But what we've learned from our own experience and from other partners is that female partnerships are more likely to succeed when partners like each other enough to invest trust, manage egos, and share control. That's why the women we interviewed consistently mentioned the relational aspects of partnership when asked to cite benefits. As we'll explore in later chapters, for women, the lure of a give-and-take relationship with a trusted colleague is a major partnership attraction. That has certainly been true for us. Our partnership took root in the tenth grade, where it provided the flexibility and inspiration for us to be creative, the freedom to be our own wacky selves, and the confidence to stand up in front of a bunch of tenth graders to present our outside-the-box approach to a school project. Since then this partnership has stretched as we've grown, shifting in sync with the stages of our lives. All the while, it has yielded tremendous benefits as we've learned to do what healthy partnerships require: listen, share, manage conflicts, take risks, support each other, and celebrate our successes.

The Next Step

For a long time, we thought the solution called partnership was the end of the story. It was making work better for us and for many other women. That was that. But as it turns out, we had only skimmed the surface. We had the solution, but we had not yet uncovered the problem. Yes, partnership is a solution that yields tremendous benefits, but why do women need these benefits? What is it about the state of women's lives that make such qualities as flexibility, confidence, freedom, support, mutual accountability, and happiness so essential? What does being a woman have to do with partnership? Stay tuned. That's the question to be explored in Chapter 2.

What Does Being Women Have to Do with It?

When we think about the power of partnership, the image that sticks in our brains is of women like you, like us, soaring side by side through the sky, leaping tall buildings in a double bound and accomplishing big things together.

What is it about female pairings that makes them dynamic duos (or trios or quartets)? What is it about partnership that brings so much freedom, so much satisfaction, such exponential power to the work lives of women? Is it because they are partners or specifically because they are women who are teaming up with other women? Are women who partner with men achieving the same results—the same freedom to be themselves, comparable confidence surges, and parallel opportunities to do the work they believe in with someone they trust? In other words, what's being a woman got to do with partnership?

Socialization or Science?

These are questions we've pondered long and hard as our thinking about power through partnership has evolved over time from a solution for women to an exploration of why such a solution is needed for women today. One potential reason partnership works so well for women is found in the work of Georgetown University linguist and best-selling author Deborah Tannen, whose research has found that women tend to see themselves as individuals in a network of connections. As Tannen describes it, "In this world, conversations are negotiations for closeness in which people try to seek and give confirmation and support, and to reach consensus. They try to protect themselves from others' attempts to push them away. Life then is a community, a struggle to preserve intimacy and avoid isolation."[13] Based on Tannen's research, partnership at its most basic level satisfies women's need to be connected and included, providing the level of closeness that Tannen cites as most meaningful.

Or could it be that partnership works so well for women because women's brains are wired to communicate and collaborate? Although brain research has stirred rigorous debates about the ethics of using science to support gender generalizations, some neuroscientists are staking their reputations on findings that qualities such as anticipating others' needs come naturally to women, making women especially likely to flourish within a tightly-woven working relationship. Neuropsychiatrist Louann Brizendine, who has studied women's brains extensively, believes that "the female brain has tremendous unique aptitudes—outstanding verbal agility, the ability to connect deeply in friendship, a nearly psychic capacity to read faces and tone of voice for emotions and states of mind, and the ability to defuse conflict. All of this is hardwired into the brains of women. These are the talents women are born with that many men, frankly, are not."[14]

Men in partnership tend to have a different approach. "Men tend to engage with the world as an individual in a hierarchical social order in which he is either one-up or one-down," Tannen observes. "In this world, conversations are negotiations in which people try to achieve and maintain the upper hand if they can, and protect themselves from others' attempts to put them down and push them around. Life, then, is a contest, a struggle to preserve independence and avoid failure."[15]

Whether it's due to the way women and men are raised, the science that makes them who they are, or some other alchemy, there are differences in the lenses, expectations, and qualities women and men bring to collaboration. Whereas men tend to bring to their collaborations a competitive energy that protects their independence and individuality, women in collaboration often find refuge from internal competition and draw energy from the connectedness partnerships allow. The premium women often place on relationships puts them in a position to contribute to and gain from the freedom, flexibility, trust, and confidence engendered in these interwoven relationships. In the eyes of many women, these qualities form the cornerstones of successful relationships: they are what distinguish a woman in collaboration from her male coworkers.

John Gerzema and Michael D'Antonio, authors of *The Athena Doctrine: How Women (and the Men Who Think Like Them) Will Rule the Future*, affirm that traditionally feminine traits such as cooperation, caring, flexibility, inclusivity, flexibility, and collaboration are the skills needed for effective, innovative leadership in the modern era. "When women combine these skills and strengths," Gerzema and D'Antonio write, "the result is often an exponential power, considerably farther reaching and with greater impact than any individual can achieve."[16] The intense give-and-take of partnership is a natural fit for the interpersonal, collaborative leadership skills women so often possess and tend to undervalue rather than appreciating them for the meaningful tools they are.

Blinders Off: Acknowledging Strengths

Before women can confidently leverage the strengths and skills they bring to collaborations, they must first acknowledge that these strengths exist and also that they are different from the qualities men bring to and value in their partnerships. This is a tough task for many women, who, like us, grew up wearing gender blinders. As proud products of the *Free to be You and Me* generation, we both were raised on the message that girls could do anything boys could do. Anything! With this kind of thinking, we grew up believing that with this fifty-fifty equality, girls and boys would surely grow to be women and men who would achieve equivalent opportunities, salaries, and power throughout their professional lives. We were raised on an assumption of gender equality. However, what was missing then is still missing today: equality and equity. These two *E*-words mean very different things but are often confused, especially when it comes to partnership.

The Inner Circle of Equality

To understand the difference between equality and equity in partnership, imagine a circle within a circle. In the inner circle, it is up to partners, regardless of gender, to determine the balance of their relationship, to decide that they want to work as full equals in a fifty-fifty collaboration that fairly balances resources, responsibility, status, respect, authority, and decision-making. In this core, partners develop relationships that are equal and take into account the full measure of each partner's needs and interests before decisions are made and actions are implemented.

The Outer Circle of Equity

Now picture the outside ring, the outer circle of equity, where the situation grows more complicated. No matter how equal the balance is in the inner circle, there's no guarantee of equity in the outer circle because this is where the world outside the partners' sphere comes into play. Equity is defined as the pay, status, access to resources, authority, and decision-making power that is conferred by forces outside partners' control.

These forces might include, but are not limited to, media, public policy, and general cultural expectations. All these forces add up to power. So another way to think of equity is a person's power as perceived by the larger society. The more perceived power a person has, the greater the equity he or she holds. And in today's world, men, especially white men, typically hold much more equity than women and thus are deferred to as the ones in power.

Not There Yet

Evergreen State College history professor and family life chronicler Stephanie Coontz summed up the current state of gender inequity, "Today the main barriers to further progress toward gender equity no longer lie in people's personal attitudes and relationships. Instead, structural impediments prevent people from acting on their egalitarian values, forcing men and women into personal accommodations and rationalizations that do not reflect their preferences."[17] In other words, as much as women and men might strive to achieve equality within their partnerships, the inequity in the larger, outer sphere works against them.

How does this tension over equity and equality affect partnerships? In the inner circle, where decisions are made by the partners themselves, any effects will depend on who is in the circle. Regardless of gender, if the partners treat each other equally and fairly, then their partnership will be equal and fair. (And if partners are not treated fairly in the inner circle, well then, we would encourage these partners to seek the nearest exit door.)

In the outer circle, equity can be a very different story, depending on the genders of the partners in the inside circle. If men are partnering together, based on gender alone, they will both be perceived as holding power. (There are other factors in the mix, but gender is the common denominator.) It's up to them to determine who holds more power.

When women and men partner, however, gender inequity comes into play. No matter how fair and balanced things are in that inner circle, women and men continue to be subject to different societal rules and expectations when it comes to who is perceived as having power and holding equity. Thus, male-female combos need to remain watchful and ready to challenge people who are not able to treat them equitably.

A recent headline in the *Huffington Post* and its telling subhead brought this home, "Business Partnerships with Men Often Don't Benefit Women; Women who start their own business would be best served by going it alone." The article explained findings from a study at the University of North Carolina at Chapel Hill, which looked at the way leadership was shared between male-female partners in small, start-up businesses. According to sociologist Tiantian Yang, "Women who start businesses with men have limited opportunities to move into leadership roles.… Men are 85 percent more likely than women to be in charge of these small business partnership start-ups."[18] The research team concluded that mixed-gender partners carry with them the cultural expectations of traditional gender roles, with men being the leaders in the public realm.

The good news is that researchers found equality could be realized if formal operating agreements with equally distributed leadership between male and female partners were in place. Without constant vigilance, however, the default mode of traditional gender roles creeps back in.

To understand what this looks like in today's work world, just consider the prevailing assumption that when a man and a woman are working together, the man is the leader. Maggie, who serves on the board of a community nonprofit, attended a regular meeting that turned into an eye-opening discussion about the prevalence of gender inequity. As board members returned to the table after a break, the chair turned to Maggie and asked why she was focusing her research on women's partnership instead of on all partnerships, regardless of gender. Maggie said, "While equality can exist within working relationships, the way that partnership is perceived by the larger world makes it challenging for true equity to exist with male-female partnerships." Maggie wasn't sure what sort of reaction to expect from this group of seasoned leaders in their forties, fifties, and sixties, and was surprised when women and men around the table began sharing their own very relevant, personal experiences.

Steve, a quiet man who worked for a financial firm co-owned equally by a female and a male partner, said his wealthy clients consistently made it clear that they expected the male partner to be at the table when it came to discussing their financial futures. Debra, the head of a high-profile Duke University management team, shared that it wasn't unusual when she was traveling with a younger male coworker for clients to look to the man as the leader. John, a senior advisor to North Carolina judges, explained that regardless of the talent, education, or high-level position of his female associates, the judges always looked to him—an older white man—first.

Maggie's takeaway from this conversation was that no matter how equal the relationship is at the center of a collaboration, when men and women partner, the male leader is the one most likely to be seen as more important in the public sphere. Imagine the long-term effects of this. As male-female partners strike an equal working relationship, their energy drains with every push against societal expectations that don't allow the equity that would truly balance their collaborations. Over time, it grows easier to allow the male partner to take the lead than to keep pushing against engrained personal habits and cultural beliefs. Sadly, these choices are often made, consciously or not, by the female partner—the one most easily diminished.

Betsy faced a similar set of compromises when she was tapped to chair a committee for a local organization. Knowing that she lacked the time to take this leadership task on alone (not to mention that partnership is her usual go-to choice), she asked Dan, a friend and respected colleague with extensive experience with the organization, to co-lead. Dan said yes, and the two of them got to work forming the committee and outlining their plan. Dan and Betsy enjoyed their work together and trusted the other to get the work done. But when they interacted with the committee or presented updates to the organization's board, there was a noticeable shift. Although the committee members were aware that Dan and Betsy were equal partners, they consistently looked to Dan first for leadership and guidance. When plans hit a snag or a bump, the community's concerns were directed to Dan. And when the process they recommended to the organization was ultimately successful, congratulations were extended to Dan.

The way Betsy saw it, she had two choices: either she could invest energy in more forcefully exerting her leadership or she could step back, allowing more time to attend to the many other things on her plate as she supported Dan. In this way, she could still lead, but more as a guest star than in the costarring role.

As far as she knows, Betsy's choice to take the supporting role didn't affect the committee or Dan. However, even though she was still involved and working, taking this backdoor approach felt like she was opting out. Betsy realized that if she had been working with a female partner and something had upset the balance between them, she would have pointed it out so that it didn't interfere with the future of their relationship or keep them from achieving goals.

Betsy's choice reflects the dynamic experienced by women throughout history: the smiling, ever-competent, supportive woman behind the dazzling man, the Lois Lane who is always there for Superman, or the Joan Harris who works with Don Draper on *Mad Men* (and who could only make partner by sleeping with a client, but that's another story). Even on *The Good Wife,* a television show that features smart, powerful women, attorney Diane Lockhart is unfavorably compared to her younger, now-deceased partner Will Gardner. These pairs might share decision-making and equality in their inner circles, but that's not what's visible to those in the outer spheres. Instead, the woman is too often ignored or relegated to a second-tier position within the partnership, the dull peahen to her partner's brilliant peacock.

Women in the Equity Circle

What happens to equity when women join forces? For starters, because no man is available to be given or to assume power, there is no automatic assumption that one person is in charge. Both partners receive the equity. And the stories shared by female partners about their collaborations brim with energy because, as the title of this book suggests, women draw power from leading together—and they need not exhaust themselves working to receive and maintain equity.

Yes, women have to work hard in partnership—no worthwhile relationship is easy. In fact, because female partners are equally accountable for contributing fully, women in partnership sometimes have to work harder or in unfamiliar areas, leaving their comfort zones to take on tasks that might traditionally default to a male partner. But they have no need to surrender or subvert power because equal power is built into the relationship. They are free to exhibit, combine, and build on their strengths, trusting that each partner is committed to growth, honesty, and giving her best to the collaboration.

The inequity we observe between women and men, in terms of society's expectations and influence on their collaborations, has led us to appreciate that the balance we have created as business partners and co-authors exists largely because we are women in collaboration—women who were raised to share, to listen, to connect deeply, and to communicate in ways that have made our partnership operate differently and more fairly than the male-female collaborations we have experienced or witnessed.

We have observed that through the freedom, flexibility, steady support, and confidence women gain through their partnerships with other women, they are working together to create cracks in that proverbial wall the gender revolution has hit. Instead of waiting for society to change and tear down the structural impediments holding women back, women in partnership are creating the structures that work for them—that allow the freedom to succeed and be themselves, and the flexibility and support needed to manage their complex lives.

We opened this chapter with an image of women soaring together, side by side. Now imagine working with a male partner who easily stands, the ground beneath his feet sure and steady, while you struggle to balance and avoid pitfalls. As you wobble, he stays upright. Of course, he's happy to put out a hand to help you, but you're tired of always having to take it. You both might yearn for equity. But there's no side-by-side flying in this scenario, just a wearying struggle to survive as you spend more and more energy resisting or surrendering to the societal forces swirling around your collaboration.

In short, there simply is nothing like having a trusted ally who is standing on the same ground, who has traveled as far, who has just as much at stake, who understands, with whom you can freely talk things out and make sense of your work and your life. From this bedrock come grace, comfort, and exponential power for women to co-lead equitably and equally. What does being women have to do with it? The answer is: everything.

Chapter 3

Debunking the Myths

We, as in human beings, all carry myths. They're dusty little boxes wedged deep in the closets of our brains, where they brim over with the truths, messages, fables, warnings, stories, and innuendos gathered throughout our lives. The sources for these myths might be lessons from parents, teachers, or role models; gossip by friends, enemies, or celebrities; messages from books, movies, advertising, or the Internet—they can come from anyone, anywhere. Over time, memories and meanings shift and grow tangled, real experiences slide into wished-for narratives, and we fill gaps with our own explanations and stories, creating and recreating our personal myths. This interwoven, barely examined part of our thinking nonetheless contributes to the fabric of who we are, casting a powerful influence—consciously or unconsciously—on our assumptions, expectations, decisions, and behavior.

When it comes to partnership, the myths that influence women's collaborations have taken root over a complex history marked on one hand by intense competition with other women for limited resources, power, access, and men, and on the other hand by the comfort women draw from the support, connection, and familiarity provided by other women in our families, communities, networks, and workplaces. From this confusing mix of facts come myths that are alive, well, and evident all around us today: queen bees and catfights, the false promises and dangers of women working together, and why it's just easier to work alone.

Women and Competition: Nice Girls, Mean Girls, and Catfights

The sense of conflict, competition, aggression, and women's fear of it is fueled in childhood, where friendships grow muddied as girls are taught to compete quietly and covertly while keeping their hands clean. Contrast this with the way boys are allowed—even encouraged—to play: loudly, physically, and messily. These contrasting worlds are breezily summed up in Helen Fielding's *Mad about the Boy*, where Bridget Jones's diary entry reads, "Quickly checked on the children. Billy was running around maniacally with a group of boys and Mabel and another small girl were cheerfully saying obscurely mean things to each other."[19] Bridget, relieved that both children are behaving as expected, returns to a furious volley of texts.

From Bridget Jones, a fictional character who considers these behaviors to be the norms for her son and daughter, to experts such as Rachel Simmons, who studied the interaction of girls in *Odd Girl Out: The Hidden Culture of Aggression in*

Girls, women are reminded that competition exists for girls and women, no matter how much they are expected to suppress it. Whereas for boys competition and aggression are considered natural parts of interaction, woven into play and ultimately into work, it's a very different story for girls. According to Simmons, "When it is expressed, the overt aggression of girls is pathologized as unfeminine or worse. Scuffles between boys, though met with swift punishment, are nevertheless seen as a predictable side effect of male adolescence. Yet, when girls fight physically, their aggression is seen as a sign of deviant behavior. This double standard has grave consequences, suggesting to girls that their aggression will be more acceptable if only they keep it indirect or covert."[20]

For many girls, aggression doesn't go away. Instead, girls learn to dole it out in ways that don't attract attention. Simmons continues, "To elude social disapproval, girls retreat beneath a surface of sweetness to hurt each other in secret. They pass covert looks and notes, manipulate quietly over time, corner one another in hallways, turn their backs, whisper and smile." From these habits emerge a culture in which girls are expected to develop other, tidy, and less visible strategies for handling the real tensions and conflicts they experience.

Women learn this aversion to conflict through experience. Audrey Nelson writes in *He Speaks, She Speaks* that the message women and men receive from society is that assertiveness and the potential for the disruption conflict can cause are "unfeminine," a label based on a long history of assumptions and expectations about women's roles and femininity. As described by Nelson, "A woman's role is to be the peacemaker, master negotiator, placater, office mom, and smoother of all ripples of conflict at work and home. Girls received the message early: sugar and spice and everything nice are the ingredients from which they are made! When a woman expresses anger she is questioned. Is this outburst hormonally driven? Is she being emotional?"[21]

With such limitations, loaded messages, and automatic hormonal assumptions, the "unfeminine" prospect of addressing conflict in anything above a whisper is understandably complex for women. In order to engage in conflict without seeming hormonal or on the brink of emotion, women have developed strategies that sugarcoat real, sparking tensions.

As girls grow into adults, they are warned to expect the workplace to be just another middle-school playground. Betsy recalls a long-ago office meeting with four female colleagues in which the conflict was at a rapid boil, though to someone who was not attuned, it probably seemed like a gentle simmer. Betsy reflects, "We were untangling the difficult power dynamics caused by one of the women in the room that had occurred over the course of a large project. But we were doing this in such a polite way that no one else who walked in—except maybe another woman—would have noticed the tension in the room. Three of us were upset with the fourth woman, who in our opinion had treated the other team members in a disrespectful, dismissive way. We were letting her know how we felt by sharing our feedback in 'feminine' ways: we exchanged niceties, smiled, and gently shared our perspectives about the poor leadership we felt the fourth woman had exercised as a team leader.

"The outcomes of this meeting were on the whole productive: four women had engaged in a conversation in which feedback was given, and four women emerged from the meeting externally unscathed, with smiles on their faces. There was no screaming, swearing, or sweating. We had quelled the conflict between us quietly and effectively." And yet, as Betsy thinks back on this moment, the image that sticks is of three women politely, quietly, covertly circling around the fourth woman and calling her to task. Although the scene was set in a conference room rather than a schoolyard, the strategies were the grown-up versions of those developed in girlhood.

In *Lean In*, Sheryl Sandberg provides context for competition in the workplace, which looms as large as or larger than competition on the schoolyard. "Women in the generations ahead of me believed, largely correctly, that only one woman would be allowed to ascend to the senior ranks in any particular company," Sandberg writes. "In the days of tokenism, women looked around the room and instead of bonding against an unfair system, they often viewed one another as competition. Ambition fueled hostility, and women wound up being ignored, undermined, and in some cases even sabotaged by other women."[22]

What's happening here? Myths based on kernels of truth from a very real history of competition are growing, producing hostility, fear, feelings of vulnerability, and widespread distrust of the female world women ordinarily look to for support. Whether the competitive arena is the home or the corner suite, this notion of women competing, fighting, undermining, and tussling with each other is more than ever a sexy media darling, worthy of prime-time coverage. As Sandburg writes, "Everyone loves a fight—and they really love a catfight. The media will report endlessly about women attacking other women, which distracts from the real issues. When arguments turn into 'she said/she said,' we all lose."[23]

The media can't seem to resist the allure of women in conflict, featuring these disputes as comedy that is awkwardly aggressive. Movies such as *Working Girl* show how mean boss Sigourney Weaver is taken down by a sweeter, younger Melanie Griffith, who not only gets the job and all its glories but captures the man as well. Current television favorites, such as *Modern Family,* pit female characters against each other in slapstick competitive settings. During a recent episode, two women competing over "best mom" status had it out with each other in a hostile game of dodgeball, whereas the male characters bonded while watching football. The twelve-year-old movie *Mean Girls,* based on Rosalind Wiseman's book *Queen Bees and Wannabees,* continues to be a cult hit for teenagers. At the end of this movie focused on exploring and exposing girl dynamics, the mean, popular girl takes a comedic splat when she's hit by a bus. She survives and learns to be kinder and gentler. *Pretty Little Liars* feeds audiences a steady stream of girl-world deception, and *The Kardashians* feature strangely alluring sisterly spats and mother-daughter psychodramas.

The catfight frenzy seems to be sticking around, at least until popular culture loses its fascination with this fantasy of women in conflict. We suspect that the fantasy is particularly captivating because women are not supposed to lose their tempers in such messy, loud ways.

But of course women lose their tempers sometimes—they are human, after all—and when it happens publicly, the gender connection is often made by observers, not by the women in conflict. For example, our friend Chris Allen, a television producer, described an argument she had with a female colleague. "It was just a normal disagreement about something minor that I can't even remember now, between two people who just happened to be women. The argument was on its way to being resolved and forgotten when a guy in the office walked by, overheard us, and hissed like a cat. By doing that, he labeled a minor argument, which someone of any gender could have had, as a catfight. He genderized it, making it worthy of office chitchat, and by doing so made us, the women in the dispute, feel diminished and humiliated." Why couldn't Chris and her colleague just have an argument without gender labeling by others?

The Complicated Girlfriend Myth: Trust or Not?

Like the catfight and mean girl myths, the girlfriend myth is alive and interfering with partnership. This myth encourages women to count on each other for a good laugh or cry, a zany adventure, a listening ear, a cathartic vent, a fun night out, and a support zone in the larger, tougher world. These friendships are modeled for women on such television shows as *Sex and the City*. The underlying theme is that without a solid circle of girlfriends to cushion them from not-so-nice women—and of course from the not-to-be-trusted men—women are just plain missing out on some of life's most essential comforts.

The fictional female partnerships we listed in the introduction reinforce this idea. These characters might not be business partners, but they are friends who, if nothing else, share meaningful connections and a surprising absence of dramatic competition between them. After all, Thelma and Louise may have driven off a cliff, but they did it together. Though Lucy and Ethel's schemes didn't accomplish what they hoped for, they always seemed happy in a ditzy sort of way. And in spite of never quite living up to a plucky theme song that promised making their dreams come true their way, Laverne and Shirley had each other, for better or for worse.

However, the girlfriend myth has another side: women must be watchful or their girlfriends might turn on them, reveal secrets, spread lies about them, try to steal attention, dates, boyfriends, husbands, jobs, or other benefits. In other words, it's OK if she's your friend, but don't trust her.

What message are we to take from this friend-or-foe history? That women do indeed need other women for comfort and support, but that friendship stretches only so far? That women should enjoy the friendship but not trust too deeply, especially when it comes to women outside their circle?

Betsy got this message as a teenager when her mother, a woman with a large circle of female friends, nonetheless warned her, as she had been warned by her mother, that girls couldn't be trusted. "Trust boys," her mother advised, "they make safer friends." While writing *Power Through Partnership*, Betsy found it hard to reconcile the mother she thought of as progressive and open-minded with the bearer of this message. Maybe it was something she'd imagined? She called to verify. "Yeah, I suppose I did say that," her mother surprised Betsy by saying. "But I don't feel that way anymore. Maybe it's because I'm past the point in life of competing with my friends. Friends can trust each other when we don't have to compete."

Betsy's mother's message carries historical weight. It's one thing for a woman to lean on another in friendship, but when it comes to getting access to needed resources, the competition can be real and fierce. This background lays the groundwork for a culture of distrust that steers women away from partnership. Women can't follow the same rules if they don't trust each other enough to play by the rules. These are the roots of stories that, like the warning Betsy received from her mother, prevent women from considering the possibility of any sort of relationship that goes beyond friendship and ventures into the scary territory of shared commitment and accountability, the very qualities partnership requires.

Moving Past the Myths

But what if the messages about women and trust were encouragements to team up together instead of warnings to stay wary? What if women, like men, had access to healthy, trust-based partnership role models? What if Carrie Bradshaw teamed up with her friends Miranda, Samantha, and Charlotte as the backers of a business venture? What if, in the movie *Working Girl*, Sigourney had said to Melanie, "Go ahead, you can have Harrison Ford. What I really want to do is partner with you and grow these ideas together!"

Even better, what if the real examples of women working together in partnerships were discovered, acclaimed, and publicized so we had living examples before us? Amy Poehler and Tina Fey have been friends for decades and have supported each other through their careers. Yet as far as we can see from interviews and media coverage, the connection between them seems to be consistently couched in personal instead of professional terms. What if Tina and Amy used their vast platforms to broadcast the power of partnership as an essential key to their success?

For hope, we can turn to Heather White and Lori Joyce, the founders of Vancouver-based "Cupcakes" and the stars of the television series *The Cupcake Girls*. Now in its third season, the Canadian reality show focuses on what it takes to be partners and best friends who are running a successful, rapidly expanding string of bakeries together and juggling lives that have involved the arrival of Lori's new baby. Because such real-life female professional partnerships already exist, it's just a matter of showcasing the trust-based collaboration at the heart of these success stories so that other women can learn what partners, such as cupcake bakers Heather and Lori, have realized. As Heather said, "So many people have said you're so lucky to have each other. Having a partner really does help at the end of the day."

Power Through Partnership

The 125 partners we interviewed are succeeding together and, like Lori and Heather, are appreciating the real benefits of partnership instead of getting caught in the myths. What these women have in common is that they are engaging in healthy, vibrant collaborations based on reciprocal trust, accountability, and commitment. They are finding ways to work through, defuse, and redirect the distracting myths that negate the power of partnership.

For example, these partners are reinvesting competitive surges between them into the outcomes of their collaborations, channeling the force that divides so many others into energy that brings them together as a united front. As Marcia Greenberger, co-founder of the National Women's Law Center, told us, it's not about pretending women don't have egos that come into play with partnership. "There is an element of ego," Greenberger explained. "While you can say it's egoless, to me it's much more of a maturity of ego." Co-founder Nancy Duff Campbell added, "Certainly there wasn't a motivation to be egoless: we want to be powerful for the institution. We wanted to develop a partnership that would work for the institution as a whole and everybody involved in it. How can we be as strong as possible and have as much influence as we can?"

Lisa Stone, Elisa Camahort Page, and Jory Des Jardins,

the co-founders of BlogHer, know a lot about influence and impact. In 2005 they started asking, "Where are the women bloggers?" and set out to bring visibility to women in the world of social media. They succeeded: BlogHer reaches 92 million viewers a month via their bloggers and social media presence.

The collaboration between these women, who described themselves to us as "pretty intense, opinionated, and confident," succeeds because, as the co-founders shared in an e-mail, "We know how to have the tough conversations, not just the easy ones. Being able to handle conflict and disagreement while remembering it's about the product, not the personalities, is very important for a long-term partnership to work. It boils down to trust. You have to have it."

These female partners know that, with trust, strong women *can* work together. The myth of the dangers that occur when strong women join forces was thoroughly debunked by the four very strong female co-founders of Peotona, a firm focused on building South Africa's infrastructure through strategic investing. These women, each a recognized national leader, were warned, by men for the most part, against the potential risk of mixing their formidable talents. Referring to Peotona's co-founders, Cheryl Carolus said, "We've all led something big in our country. When we came together to form Peotona, there was a lot of skepticism from men—sexism that strong women can't stand other strong women. We knew women work together differently when they all bring their own strengths to the table, and we saw this as a safe haven. While we have all been leaders of big things that other women haven't done before, we've also made it without behaving badly, without stabbing each other to death with our stilettos."

Most of all, these partners know what it takes to make a real partnership. While they value the strong ties at the core of their collaborations, they respect the wide gulf between what it takes to be a friend and what it takes to be a co-leader. Nicola Kraus, who with her writing partner, Emma McLaughlin, wrote *The Nanny Diaries* and several other novels, drew the line between friendship and partnership when she warned that a business partnership is not a natural extension of a shopping and eating friendship. "You are forming a business relationship, not just meeting for brunch," Emma made clear. This intentional drawing of lines matters in female collaborations, in which a high value is typically placed on the relationship at the core.

Are Myths Keeping Women's Partnerships Invisible?

With all these powerhouse examples, why is it that when women think of partnership, or when Google does, these hard-working, wildly-achieving partnerships don't appear? Why are women's collaborations still traveling under the radar? And why aren't these partners, who know how closely collaboration is linked to their success, broadcasting the exponential benefits of collaboration?

Maybe these partners are wary of media that are more

interested in the entertainment value of catfights than in help-ing women find new and better ways of working. Or perhaps the answer can be connected to the feminine tendency to pre-fer investing energy in working rather than in boasting about achievements. These partners might chalk up their experiences to good luck, as we once did, or they haven't taken the next step to imagine that other women might benefit from this model. A theme many partners shared in our interviews is that they were not asked about their partnerships, perhaps because stories about women working well together don't create sexy media.

Whatever the reasons—no doubt there are many, and they are interconnected—the result is that the very women who are in the best position to proclaim the powers of part-nership are not doing so. Not yet.

But That Can Change

Who can make the change happen? These partners can, we can, and you can, by celebrating real partnerships as viable models and debunking partnership-blocking myths. We must dig deep into our myths to find the simple truth that we are better together. And then we can expand this truth to allow women to be there for each other through thick and thin not only as friends but also as co-leaders. In good times and bad, women already turn to each other for support, empathy, confidence boosts, laughter, and occasional casseroles. Why shouldn't it also be obvious that, when personal and professional boundaries are clearly marked, women need not limit these relationships to friendship? Women can invest their trust in each other and can share the accountability and commitment needed to fulfill passions and achieve professional dreams as well.

Whether she is a sister, mother, friend, or colleague, women are there for each other to celebrate the ups and figure out how to deal with the downs. Instead of letting myths block the possibilities of partnership, let's explore and broadcast more opportunities for joining forces. That's what we want women (and Google) to know!

Chapter 4

Searching for Partners

You have debunked the myths and are intrigued by the possibilities that open up to women who are working together: numerous benefits, seemingly limitless opportunities, and vast potential. But one pesky question keeps popping up, dampening your enthusiasm and sticking a pin in your dreams: Who will you partner with?

You see the advantages of intentional collaborations and are eager to share the load with an equal partner with whom you can exchange ideas, celebrate successes, and shoulder the losses—someone who will share accountability, responsibility, and risk to achieve outcomes together. But you also understand that this important relationship will demand a lot from both you and your partner. She can't be just anyone—this has to be right. And you have no idea who that right someone might be. In this chapter, we will help you figure that out.

The first thing you should know is that you're not alone. Finding a partner can be daunting for both men and women, but for women it is even more difficult because they are looking for more. We have observed that men tend to be straight-forward in their collaborations, focused on moving from actions to results. Their relationships may be important, but they don't seem to carry the same weight as relationships do in female partnerships.

Betsy's recent conversation with her friend Alice exemplifies the difference. Alice's husband, Fred, had worked with his writing partner for years—they had co-authored a book that made quite a splash, flying off the shelves and receiving rave reviews. By male standards, these partners had accomplished their goals and achieved success. It didn't seem to matter to either partner that they didn't enjoy working together. What mattered was that one partner brought subject matter expertise, and the other was a recognized writer with an impressive platform. Neither partner particularly liked or trusted the other, but both saw the collaboration as a means to an end, a partnership that had to be endured, at least for the time being. Binding legal contracts dealt with the mistrust and protected each partner. Feelings were beside the point.

Betsy and Alice realized that this model wouldn't work for most women, who typically count on a significant degree of connection to make their collaborations work. Our partnership research also strongly supports the finding that in women's partnerships, feelings are central. As aerialist Amanda Leoni of Down to Earth Acrobats said about her year-old partnership with Amy Cherico, "I don't want to sound sexist or generalize all women into one category; I just think it's rare that women can mix business and friendship successfully without the emotional element. It's not something to be ashamed of, it's just something to recognize and address so when the puppy love of new partnership wears off, you can still be successful."

Whereas men might see collaboration as a means to an end, the women partners we've talked with often find that much of the satisfaction they receive from collaboration comes from these trust-based relationships. The takeaway here is that finding a partner is a weighty task because women are willing to contribute to and expect to find a relationship that's far more intricate than a straightforward business transaction. For Fred and his partner, the relationship paled in light of the outcomes; for many women, a fractured relationship would hinder or halt the outcomes of the work.

Knowing that relationships assume a starring role in women's partnerships can make finding the "right" partner can seem like a daunting prospect. In fact, more than half of the partners we interviewed compared work partnership with marriage. However, although marriage might be the closest metaphor we have to describe the commitment and closeness of an ongoing business partnership, these professional relationships and and marriage are not synonymous. When women choose work partners, they are not looking for the equivalent of a spouse with whom they make a life-long commitment. In partnership, instead of a vow to stay together "till death do you part," there's a shared commitment to getting the work done together to accomplish shared goals and achieve a mutual vision. Once these objectives are fulfilled, it is possible for healthy partnerships to shift, stretch, or end—without the emotions tied to marital transitions.

Starting the Search by Looking at Yourself

In work relationships that are this interwoven, the expectations and assumptions partners unknowingly bring to collaboration can easily blur the line between the professional and the personal in ways that hinder rather than enhance outcomes. We all have baggage, from tidy little tote bags to sacks. What's inside might be a complicated mix of the myths we explored in Chapter 3: past experiences, assumptions, expectations, dreams, and hopes. To avoid this trap, we strongly recommend that you take stock of the hopes and hang-ups you bring to the partnership. What kinds of experiences, memories, ideals, and assumptions are you hauling along with you? When you take the time to unpack your luggage before hauling it into your partnership, you will enter the relationship as a clear-eyed, self-aware partner who knows what she wants from partnership and why.

What Do You Want and Need?

When you are clear about your necessities and desires, you will be much more likely to find what you are looking for. That's the lesson we learned from Marirose Steigerwald, who in her search for the perfect job held on to the five things she needed and longed for: (1) a leadership position; (2) to leverage the many skills she had developed over a long, diverse career; (3) to have fun at work; (4) to work with people she could laugh with; and (5) to work in a beautiful place.

After making painful decisions to turn down some near-perfect opportunities that didn't meet all five of her criteria, Marirose heard through the grapevine that Patti Gillenwater was looking for a partner to help lead Elinvar, a boutique search and coaching firm—that happened to be located in a gorgeous old Raleigh, North Carolina mansion! It didn't take long for Marirose to realize that this opportunity satisfied all her criteria. But first she had to clarify just what those items were.

For Lisa Wojnovich, it took just one surprising answer to an unexpected question to lead her to partnership. Before starting the children's custom art business, Litsy Designs, with friend and fellow artist Patsy Smith, Lisa was a new mother with a public health background who participated in a dream workshop. When the facilitator asked, "What would you do if you knew you couldn't fail?" Lisa was surprised by her own response, "Be a famous artist." In that moment, Lisa, who loved drawing and painting but had never seriously considered becoming an artist, made the bold decision to pursue her dreams.

Once she had the idea about turning her artistic pursuits into a business, Lisa reflected on her previous work experience and realized that she was most productive when she had someone with whom to discuss ideas and develop action plans. She recognized that in order to bring her ideas to life, she needed the mutual accountability of a partner to help set and follow through on goals.

What to Look for in a Partner

Once Lisa realized what she was bringing to and what she wanted from a partnership, she had a clearer sense of what to look for in a potential partner. When she realized she needed someone who was both creative and business savvy, she immediately thought of Patsy Smith, an entrepreneurial neighbor with a background in merchandising and retail. According to Lisa, "I enlisted Patsy, who I knew was super creative and probably wouldn't say no!" She was right. Although they didn't know each other well, Patsy was just as eager to dip her toes into a partnership project. Lisa and Patsy decided to launch their business by creating and selling whimsical nameplates at a local street fair. The street fair introduction was a hit, and Lisa and Patsy went on to establish Litsy Designs. Litsy's success boomed after the hit television show *Gray's Anatomy* started featuring their designs as background art.

Three Essentials for Finding the Right Partner

How did Lisa and Patsy know that they had found the right partner? After talks with female partners, we can happily say there's a lot more to it than luck. What Patsy and Lisa found in each other are three qualities: (1) complementary skills, talents, and interests; (2) shared values; and (3) compatibility.

We want to focus on these essentials because they were consistently mentioned by partners in our interviews and because we believe these qualities form the basis for successful working partnerships between women. This is not to downplay the importance of such traditional business metrics as ample resources, infusions of capital, strategic goals, solid revenue projections, and partnership agreements. These concrete aspects of business certainly matter, but they are covered in many other resources.

When we asked female partners to describe what was most important in their collaborations, we heard such responses as how good it felt to know their dream was possible when they merged complementary skills, how much it meant to have the chance to put values into action with a trusted colleague, and the great joy they received from working with their partner. As we saw in Chapter 1, women tend to factor in the relational aspects when they calculate the benefits in, and success of, a partnership or other work experience. (Our hunches tell us that the priorities may be different for men.)

It's Complementary, My Dear Partner

The search for complementary skills plays a central role in Lisa and Patsy's story. Lisa was looking for someone who had the business and merchandising savvy she lacked. For Patsy, Lisa's energy (or, as Lisa described it, her tendency to be an "idea hamster") was the yin to Patsy's yang. By bridging their skills, Lisa and Patsy developed a business in which both partners could apply their strengths, knowing that the full balance of their skills made it possible to achieve the goals both were committed to fulfilling.

Before starting a business, project, or endeavor of any sort, both partners need to honestly inventory their own skills and gaps. Coworkers turned co-founders Amy Gonzalez and Kelly Caldwell, of the environmental engineering and construction firm AK Environmental, seized the opportunity to go forth and partner while at dinner one night after a long day in the field. Seasoned veteran Amy was ready to go out on her own. She had put the time in, had the know-how and contacts, but her big thinking about running her own company was dampened by the realities of having to manage her own finances. That's where then-protégé Kelly immediately saw the chance to collaborate. "I'll balance the checkbook," said Kelly, and with that a partnership that masterfully leverages diverse skills was born. With a three-year growth rate of 844 percent, a cover story in *INC.* magazine, and a recent ranking of #6 in the Top 50 Fastest-Growing Women-Led Companies in North America,[24] obviously Amy and Kelly are doing many things right. But they wouldn't be where they are today without that alchemy of complementary skills.

Kelly and Amy knew their skills were complementary by the roles each assumed in their past and current companies. How will you know if you and your partner have complementary skills? It's as simple as watching your prospective partner in action, asking thoughtful questions and listening carefully to the answers, and understanding exactly what skills your entity needs to be successful. Business writer Margaret Heffernan put it bluntly when we interviewed her via Skype from her home in England, "If the partner is just like you, then one of you doesn't need to be there."

Shared Values

Whereas skills may be different but fit like puzzle pieces, forming a cohesive whole, values work best for partnerships when they are shared so they can provide a firm guide for decisions and direction.

Values are the beliefs you carry about what matters to you and why. A strong business model reflects these values, and an effective collaboration, regardless of gender, bridges these values so that partners are combining strengths to pursue the values they are jointly committed to fulfill.

Remember Cheryl Carolus, Dolly Mokgatle, Thandi Orleyn, and Wendy Lucas-Bull, the founders of Peotona, a South African investment company? These anti-apartheid activists, who were part of the team that helped Nelson Mandela win the first democratic election, believe so strongly in the economic future of their country that they left other successful careers to unite. Through their leadership of Peotona, the partners have made a collective commitment to channel their shared passion into rebuilding the infrastructure of South Africa. Peotona's co-leaders came together after each had demonstrated these values as a respected South African leader in her own right. The previous knowledge of each other's values and the mutual respect they inspired formed the starting point for extensive values-focused conversations among the partners. According to Wendy Lucas-Bull, "We spent quite a bit of time when we started in fleshing out what we wanted in values and what we wanted aspirationally to do and the kind of things not to do."

Paying close attention to the values that underscore Peotona is what unites the partners: each knows she is in the company of others who are as committed to creating positive change for South Africa as she is. These values, woven into Peotona's mission and vision, have grown beyond any individual partner as they inspire employees and stakeholders to work together to build the nation's infrastructure.

A Cautionary Tale about Values

What if you discover the partner you thought was ideal actually isn't in sync with your values after all? While traveling in San Francisco, we struck up a train-ride conversation with Claudia, a former co-founder of a healthcare IT start-up who heard us talking about *Power Through Partnership* and offered her own partnership story. Claudia and her former partner bridged complementary skills and styles to develop a competitive nonprofit company that took off in a relatively short time. In the midst of fast-paced growth, the partners found themselves swamped as they led their separate spheres. Their values about managing and structuring the organization began to differ, particularly around organizational culture, delegation of responsibility, and client priorities. Ultimately, Claudia realized the partnership no longer worked for her or the organization she had started, and it was time for her to separate and start a solo consulting practice. Claudia emphasized the importance of recognizing when partnerships stop working.

Are Complementary Skills and Shared Values Enough?

Let's say you are considering a partnership with a colleague. You've seen her at work, and you know your skills blend perfectly—she's an ace with numbers and you're a strategy maestro. Together you have a solid foundation for building a strategic consulting practice. You also know that you share similar values about achieving balanced personal and professional lives. You are equally passionate about helping nonprofit service agencies grow and fulfill their missions. It seems perfect!

But what if you really don't like each other? Of all the people you could spend time with, she's pretty much the last one you'd choose (and you're pretty sure the feeling is mutual). Can such a partnership survive? Chances are the answer is no. You lack compatibility.

Compatibility

It might not seem like the end of the world if you don't want to spend time together and don't enjoy each other's company. But what we've seen in many women's partnerships is that compatibility counts for a lot. In sharp contrast with the story about Alice's husband, Fred, and his partner, whose successful collaboration clearly did not click, women need to like each other. They need camaraderie as well as respect and trust for these intensive relationships to work.

Before we go any farther, please note that we said like, not love. Yet another distinction from matrimony is that love doesn't have to be part of the equation. Partners don't need to be best friends, or even be good friends. Sometimes the strongest partnership relationship is purely professional. You don't have to socialize or chitchat with your partner, but you do need to enjoy a level of camaraderie.

We'd be remiss if we didn't wave a caution flag here. There's obviously more to healthy partnerships than just liking your partner: if that's all it took, your list of possible partners might be ten times longer. What works in friendship doesn't necessarily transfer to partnership because the risks in partnership are many times greater. We have heard many stories about partners who, blinded by camaraderie, glossed over other essentials and ended up with unfulfilled goals and dysfunctional relationships.

Can Friends Work as Partners?

This brings us to the big partnership question: Can friends partner? Our answer is a resounding yes! In fact, because we were friends first, we once believed that partners were better off if they had a preexisting friendship to build on. What we've come to realize, though, is that partnership works for women, friends-first or not, if they share the same commitment to doing the heavy lifting it takes to make partnerships work. In some ways, this is easier for friends-first partners because the trust is already there. And in many other ways it's a lot harder, because partners must be able to have honest, tough conversations about money, values, and goals that friends sometimes aren't comfortable having.

As we know from our own collaboration, when you are friends first you need to work hard to preserve your preexisting relationship by establishing boundaries between work and play. Your professional venture might bring you closer or it might push you apart, depending on how you handle the conflicts and challenges that arise. Taking the time up front to talk through scenarios and establish a partnership agreement is important for all new partnerships—for friends or new acquaintances.

Other friends-first partners—including Amy Rae and Emily Saliers of the Indigo Girls, internationally acclaimed singer-songwriters who first met in the high school chorus; Caryn Levine and Julie Kepniss, of Hitched; and the Cupcake Girls' Lori Joyce and Heather White—shared similar themes. Each set of partners was well aware of the risks of working with a friend, while at the same time each was enormously grateful to have such a close friend with whom to work.

The friendship shared by Valerie Batts and Angela Bryant, co-founders of VISIONS, Inc., a multicultural consulting and community-development practice, goes so far back they're practically family. There's even a picture of them as babies, born just six months apart, in the same crib. But this closeness hasn't guaranteed ease in their partnership. "We're exact opposites in the Myers-Briggs Type Indicator,®" Angela explained. "I want to consider all possibilities and Valerie wants to decide and move on. Val feels like it's OK if things are a little fuzzy. I like detail, but Val will think it's too much."

What makes this friendship-based partnership of opposites work are the clear roles the partners have assumed over their decades-long co-leadership. According to Angela, "When our roles are clear, differences are easier to work with. In our consulting work, Val's role is to lead and mine is to follow. I have had to become satisfied with that. In the community-development arm of the business, I take the lead." It's Angela and Valerie's strong and sturdy relationship at the center that keeps them connected, regardless of who is leading and who is following. As Valerie said, "Nothing is more important than knowing Angela is there. This is what makes it worth working out, no matter whatever happens in the world. We fell in love with each other as children and our attachment holds everything together."

What about Virtual Strangers?

We have received almost as many questions from women about whether it works to team up with women they don't know well. Our answer to this is also an emphatic yes! The funny part is that in our interviews, we often heard from friends-first partners that partnership couldn't or wouldn't work any other way. Partners had to know each other well in order to fully trust each other and share control. And we heard exactly the opposite from women who didn't know each other before they started collaborating. These women expressed gratitude at the chance to build a relationship from scratch.

Ann Patchett and Karen Hayes, of Nashville's Parnassus Books, met over a lunch coordinated by a mutual friend and decided within twenty-four hours to co-lead the independent book shop, with Ann as the funder and Karen as the operations manager. When we asked Ann and Karen about the risks of working with virtual strangers, Ann reiterated the advantages of building a partnership from scratch versus retrofitting a previous relationship into a professional collaboration. As Ann put it, "I remember thinking when we started out how hard it would be if I was doing this with my best friend. I would feel guilty about not being in the store more. Starting fresh as partners means you don't necessarily have to unlearn roles that aren't serving the business well."

These contrasting perspectives between friends-first partners and virtual-stranger partners tell us two things: (1) that partners are so satisfied with their work together they can't imagine it any other way; and (2) what matters in partnership is that, whatever the relationship before partnership, success is most likely when partners are committed to doing the communicating, trusting, sharing, working, and leading it takes to make the partnership work.

Of course, as Karen and Ann can attest, entering a partnership with someone you don't know requires its own level of caution. Whereas friends-first partners must take care to preserve their friendships, virtual strangers need to do their homework to ensure they are making grounded decisions about entering collaboration. Karen and Ann's decision to partner might have been quick, but it was made on the solid recommendation of a trusted and reliable third party and only after the pair clarified their responsibilities.

Keeping It in the Family

The stew of family-based partnerships has the same base but is slightly thicker and spicier than the friendship variety. Although the family option isn't for everyone, when it works, it really works. After all, nobody knows you like your mother, sister, daughter, or your life partner. What does it take for family members to effectively and graciously share the leadership helm? In addition to seeing each other as equals, sorting through the baggage, moving past the history, being honest, communicating, and respecting each other. As equal professionals, family partners may need to break familial patterns and hierarchies to accept partnership roles and form new relationships with clear boundaries.

According to Piper Kessler and Monique Velasquez, life partners and co-owners of Velasquez Digital Media, "Work and life are all mixed up." As Monique shared, "The difference between life partners and business partnerships is that as business partners we have had lots of forced conversations about what we want to do for the future, how we want to proceed over the next three to five years, and how these things affect our home life." With life weaving into work and work into life,

Monique and Piper needed to strategically plan for the futures of both their work and their life partnerships by figuring out how their relationship at work shifts once they go home. According to Piper, "At work Monique is the boss. I shift gears. And at home it's more equal." Like VISIONS Inc.'s Angela and Valerie, for Monique and Piper, the clear roles that work for both of them keep their partnership tight at home and at work.

For mother-daughter team Gladys Gonzalez and Sandra Gonzalez who worked closely to create *Mundo Hispáno*, the first Spanish-language newspaper in Utah, partnership meant building from the strength of their relationship to adapt to the needs of their growing business. As immigrants from Colombia, Gladys and Sandra relied heavily on each other for support when they came to the United States in the early 1990s. When Gladys decided Utah needed a paper for its growing Latino population, she turned to Sandra, who has a background in journalism.

When asked to describe some challenges of working together as family members, Gladys commented, "The hardest part has been keeping a unified vision and being flexible to change according to the needs of the company. It used to be difficult for me to be flexible. I held on to the role of being in charge as a mother. Sandra taught me the importance of having a wider perspective and making changes." Family members who choose to work together, such as Gladys and Sandra, need to consider the potential difficulties of surrendering a familiar position and status to work in new roles. Just because you're the one in charge at home doesn't mean you're the best person to be the CEO at work.

Consider the Competition

When you begin to think about finding a partner, you might not immediately consider looking among women considered to be your professional competition. But think of the expanded network of contacts, clients, and customers that could be created from collaboration between competitors. This was the case for Linda Kaplan Thaler and Robin Koval, co-founders of New York's Kaplan Thaler advertising agency and co-authors of several books, including *The Power of Nice,* who, like bookstore owners Ann Patchett and Karen Hayes, were brought together by a mutual colleague, in this case their client, the CEO of Clairol.

In another example, Laura Matalon and Tanya Grubich, the founders of The Marketing Group, joined forces after years of competing behind the scenes and sets of Broadway. As Tanya said, "If we hadn't partnered, we would have been competing against each other. Instead, by working together, we cornered the market." Laura added, "Between us we have 90 percent of the relationships required in the industry and are able to capitalize on those." It's important to note that while these women were in competitive organizations, none had any reason to internalize the competition or feel threatened by it; therefore, the ability to trust was not endangered.

Partners Are Everywhere

Among the women we interviewed, partners found each other at work, on playgrounds, through matchmakers, in their own families, at schools, and via volunteer gigs. Our research has convinced us that just as there's no one right partner, there's no one right way to find a partner. If you keep your eyes open and know what you're looking for, you just might find a partner in an unlikely place.

Mari Lazar and Kate Tempesta, co-founders of the Kate Tempesta Urban Golf Academy in New York City, met when Mari signed her daughters up for the golf class Kate was teaching in Central Park. Maryanne Perrin and Kella Hatcher, co-founders of Balancing Professionals, a staffing firm that advocated for flexible work options, and Christa Granderson-Reid and Janai Nelson, of Brownstone Buddies (multicultural dolls), met their respective partners in neighborhood playgrounds with their young children in tow.

Our most unlikely partners, food writer Kelly Alexander and researcher-librarian Cynthia Harris, met when Kelly showed up in snowy Kansas wearing her high New York City heels to meet and, ultimately, collaborate on an article about Clementine Paddleford, a beloved but long-forgotten food writer and cultural chronicler. The duo's shared passion for re-igniting Paddleford's legacy inspired a ten-year collaboration, a James Beard Award, and their book, *Hometown Appetites: The Story of Clementine Paddleford, the Forgotten Food Writer Who Chronicled How America Ate.*

Is It "Just Right"?

It's not scientific and it's far from concrete, but for the women we talked with, often the best indicator of a healthy partnership was the "just-right" feeling they got from their partner. If you don't feel that the fit is exactly right, do yourself and your potential partner a favor and stop right there.

Jodi Thompson of Results-Only Work Environment had been in a partnership with two other women before she founded ROWE with Cali Ressler, and it didn't go so well. "Trust your gut; it's a great compass," she told us. "With my business partners before, something in my gut told me 'this isn't right, move on,' and I ignored those red flags, and it failed. You want it to work so badly that sometimes you ignore these things." Learn from Jodi, and trust your instincts.

For our friend Perri Kersh, it was her gut response that told her she was ready for partnership after resisting the idea for years. Although she liked the idea of sharing the load of leading Neat Freak, the home-organizing company she'd created from scratch, she didn't know who she could trust to care as much about the company as she did. When Perri had some new opportunities that stretched her solo capacity, she knew it was time to reconsider partnership. Perri told us, "I had been working alone as a professional organizer for close to six years when I realized it was time to grow. In addition to being a Neat Freak, I'm also a bit of a control freak, so inviting someone else to work with me felt unnerving. I was hired to tackle a couple of large jobs that I knew I could handle more successfully with an extra set of hands and an extra organizing brain. And I also knew I didn't have the skills to do some of the technical work some clients were asking for."

Once Perri recognized this need, the answer to who could be a partner came surprisingly quickly: who else but her long-time friend and reliable colleague Mary Beth Grealey? Perri and Mary Beth were friends who had already worked together for a number of years, they cohosted the Giving Party, a holiday fund-raiser that supports local nonprofits. Plus they had served on church committees and worked together at their children's preschool. For Perri, "I never even considered bringing anyone else on board! I knew she would be fun to work with, I could trust her completely, and that she would add to what we could offer our clients. And I'm not at all surprised to realize that all of that has come true as we've now worked together for a little over three years."

It didn't take long for Mary Beth to agree, and she hasn't looked back. She said, "Perri and I have so much fun together, and we haven't yet run into a project that can't be conquered with humor and hard work. We are each other's biggest fan, and she's usually my first call with news of any kind. As I work with clients, being able to discuss challenges and successes with Perri helps me learn and move forward. Her work and personal experience is valuable to me professionally, but her friendship keeps me grounded."

Since teaming up, Perri and Mary Beth have learned to balance the load, support each other, and play to their strengths. When we asked Perri how, after being doubtful about potential partners for so long, she'd known Mary Beth was the right one, she said, "It's kind of like Mary Beth was in my mind the whole time—waiting to partner. Suddenly, I just knew it was right."

That just-right feeling is what happens when you've done the thinking, prepping, and strategizing needed for partnership. Sometimes it's purposeful, finding a partner. Other times, as in Perri and Mary Beth's case, it's in the wings of your mind, just waiting for the ideal opportunity. Whenever, however it happens, pay attention and resist that ingrained urge to say, "Never mind. I'll just do it myself." Being able to do it yourself is beside the point. The real question is why should you when you can lead side by side in a professional relationship with a sister, mother, friend, coworker, competitor, or playground acquaintance you like, trust, and respect?

Chapter 5

Preparing for Risks

When we met our friend Gina for lunch, she couldn't wait to update us about her videography business. It had grown immensely since we'd last seen her, and now it was generating more work than Gina could handle on her own. Her excitement was obvious as she shared the news that she was considering formalizing a partnership with a woman with whom she had recently collaborated on a documentary project. Then, seemingly out of nowhere, her tone grew somber. "I just don't think I can do it," she said. "What if I let her down? What if she lets me down? What if I can't give up control? What if she can't?"

We've heard Gina's fears about the risks of partnership echoed by many women. Yes, women worry about money and failure and other common perils. But those concerns are wrapped up in the fear that surfaces when you hitch your wagon to a respected peer's: your failure is hers, her mistakes are yours, and the anticipated weight of accountability seems impossibly heavy. We couldn't tell Gina that partnership would be easy or risk-free or that she and her partner would never disappoint each other. But we could tell her that these are not the greatest risks.

The Greatest Risk

What partners in healthy collaboration are finding is that "the greatest risk is no partnership at all." That's how Jody Thompson, co-founder of workplace innovator Results-Only Work Environments (ROWE), put it when we asked her to describe the risks of partnership. Her business partner, Cali Ressler, added, "The risk is that if we didn't do this together, ROWE wouldn't be here right now. I can't even believe this accomplishment; we transcended so many levels in such a short period of time." Through partnership, women like Cali and Jody have progressed in far-reaching, invigorating ways. In the process they have done the opposite of letting themselves down: they have succeeded and driven their business forward.

Risk as Motivator

Jody and Cali aren't the only ones. In our interviews, many partners noted that the risks partnership allows are potential assets—or at least enticing challenges. They also point out that seeing risks as opportunities instead of threats is a more inviting and exciting approach for partners when they launch and lead new ventures together. In partnership, the weighty sense of accountability that can wear women down becomes a boon, a motivator for partners to do their best for each other.

Once in partnership, these women don't need to anguish over whether the risk to be taken is foolish—or worse, selfish. They don't need to fret over whether they are letting others down. Once they've made the commitment to partner, what matters is that they are accountable for achieving a shared vision that is larger than both of them.

As Linda Kaplan Thaler, of Kaplan Thaler, explained, "One of the great things about partnership is the guilt factor—you don't want to let your partner down. I didn't want to let myself down, but I really didn't want to let Robin down. I'm sure it was the same for her. It's really important. You motivate each other." By channeling fear and guilt into accountability, these partners are transforming fear into strength that inspires them as individuals and fortifies their partnership.

Linda's comment sheds light on an irony in women's partnerships. Some women resist partnership because of the accountability it requires. Yet what we and other women partners, such as Linda, Cali, and Jody, have found is that the opposite is true. The shared accountability is a powerful motivator and a key benefit of collaboration. With clear commitment and shared responsibility to doing the work required, healthy partnerships are the ideal places to take risks and try new things in order to fulfill visions and honor commitments.

Perhaps if Gina had realized this fact, she would have been able to move forward with partnership, trusting herself and her potential partner to share accountability and control. Instead, her fears blocked what could have been a brilliant collaboration, leaving her holding down the fort alone. Not making the leap to partnership has meant that Gina hasn't been able to take on bigger, more exciting projects. Even though she has filled the gaps by hiring temporary contract employees, she has missed out on the exponential effects of expanding the reach of her new business with a partner who shares her vision and commitment.

Talk Therapy

Early in our research, we traveled to California to interview movie producers Marian Rees and Anne Hopkins. Their long and productive collaboration is a testament to what can result when partners plunge into risk and keep on swimming. When Marian and Anne decided to leave comfortable but dead-end jobs in male-dominated 1970s television to establish their own film production company, they knew an uphill battle awaited them. But they were ready for it.

After working diligently for fifteen years for Norman Lear and other male-owned partnerships, Marian realized she was never going to get the equity in the work that was her due. When she was blatantly passed over for a promotion, she knew she had gone as high as she could go in that world. So she headed off on her own, mortgaging her car and her house to launch Marian Rees and Associates. Marian's bold move inspired her colleague Anne Hopkins to leave her position and join forces with Marian. Many years later, as she reflected on those early days, Anne remarked, "I believed in what Marian was doing. She started with a dream, shared values, and a need for equity."

Forty years and a long list of movies later, the pair attributes their success to their shared courage in the face of risk. After a day on the set of their latest film, we settled into the producers' trailer for a rich discussion. "Underneath the history of our partnership is the awareness of risk," Marian said in her timbered voice. "For film producers like us who went out on our own as we did, risk-taking had to be fundamental. But for many women risk-taking on that level ignites fear. To mitigate our own fear, we learned to talk it through with each other, which has allowed us to listen to a voice other than our own."

Marian and Anne have learned from experience that risk-taking can stir up a range of fears—from not being accountable to being let down—but just as significantly, they've learned how to really communicate with each other, a process that involves both talking and listening.

Imagining Scenarios

This gift of talk—that is, sharing, listening, planning, thinking, and puzzling things through—is how we started our own collaboration. Before officially launching Mulberry, we spent hours thinking through endless "what-if" scenarios while our infant daughters napped in the next room. We hoped that our ability to candidly address scary possibilities would make it possible, though certainly not easy, to face these situations if they arose. We also took the time to imagine fantastic possibilities—success beyond our wildest dreams. Back then, we thought we were laying the groundwork for our business. What we realize now is that the shared responsibility and commitment to Mulberry that emerged were actually the life-lines of a strong partnership. We wouldn't let our partnership go because we both deeply felt we owed it to each other to sustain it through the best and worst of times. This was our version of Linda Kaplan Thaler's "guilt factor."

Four years later, a what-if that wasn't part of our scenario planning challenged our partnership: Maggie was diagnosed with leukemia, rocking our worlds and bringing our partnership to a grinding halt. As Maggie made sense of new personal realities and coped with medications that wreaked havoc on every part of her body, Betsy, suddenly a solo act, struggled to keep The Mulberry Partners afloat while worrying intensely about the health of her close friend. Before Maggie's diagnosis, our collaboration was a well-oiled machine. Afterward, all bets were off as we examined and reevaluated priorities we had long taken for granted.

Medicine saved Maggie; targeted therapy turned what was once a fatal disease into a chronic, treatable condition. What saved our partnership was the talking and listening we had done throughout, from our early planning discussions to the many tough conversations we shared in the months after Maggie's diagnosis, in which we reexamined our priorities and ultimately reaffirmed our original commitment to leading The Mulberry Partners and sustaining our collaboration.

If we had known while sitting at Maggie's kitchen table in the early days of our collaboration what was coming our way, would we have still joined forces? Although we can only speculate about the past, we imagine the answer is yes. We may have entered partnership eagerly, but we sure didn't enter it lightly. Those hours spent planning didn't necessarily prepare us for the specifics of what was to come, but they did help us think through future possibilities. Rather than turning away from the what-ifs we were visualizing in these scenarios, we faced them, from the most exciting vision of success to the scariest threat of failure, and we used them as the basis of the partnership agreements we later formalized.

The What-If Trap

Although thinking through possible scenarios is an important preparation for future risk planning, we caution partners against getting stuck in the trap of the what-if. On one hand, fearing and avoiding what-if discussions can leave a partnership unprepared and headed for failure. As *The Power of Two* co-author Isabel Yuriko Stenzel Byrnes wisely put it, "Advance care planning won't make you die. Talking about sex won't make you pregnant. Talking about what might happen someday, including the ending of the business or the partnership, won't bring it about any sooner." In other words, the mere act of planning won't cause whatever is dreaded.

On the other hand, overstressing possible negative outcomes can cut off potential positives outcomes before they can become real. In *Lean In*, Sheryl Sandberg devotes an entire chapter to the inclination of professional women to pull back from leadership challenges because of what might be in their future many years down the line. "I'm a big believer in thoughtful preparation," Sandberg writes. "But when it comes to integrating career and family, planning too far in advance can close doors rather than open them. I have seen this happen over and over. Women rarely make one big decision to leave the workforce. Instead, they make a lot of small decisions along the way, making accommodations and sacrifices that they believe will be required to have a family. Of all the ways women hold themselves back, perhaps the most pervasive is that they leave before they leave."[25]

This fear is activated when women consider joining forces with other women (we imagine the same is true for men). While working together might sound good, what-ifs can prevent deliberation and realistic assessment, blocking the path to partnership before plans become concrete.

And yet partnership is so often a solution for the most paralyzing what-ifs. Author Ann Patchett's decision to buy a bookstore with Karen Hayes, a friend of a friend, could have been hampered by the fear of the unknown. As Ann shared in a magazine interview after her conversation with us, "Small businesses are great, but they're also sort of terrifying. It was a little like jumping off a cliff in the dark, but you know what? I landed on my feet." What made her jump possible? According to Ann, "I have to say the most important fact in this whole story is my business partner. The deal is that Karen manages the store, works there all the time, and I paid for the store and promote it." [26] In Ann's case, her fear of risk and of what might happen was mitigated by her partnership with Karen and the clear focus both women bring to their very different roles. [26]

Ann and Karen's successful collaboration is based on the great amount of trust each places in the other to fulfill her role. During her interview with us Ann suggested, "Work with someone you respect and don't micromanage them. Find someone you feel will do a great job and don't breathe down their neck. I'm a big believer in division of trust. It goes back to the amazing extent of how we don't work together. We trust each other. I have complete blanket trust and confidence in Karen. I would never consider getting into what I consider her business."

Allowing this degree of trust to flow requires a certain loss of control, a scary prospect identified by our friend Gina. Women who prefer tight control will need to loosen the reins, move over, and make space for a copilot. Otherwise, the result is not a partnership but a hierarchy. For many partners—certainly for Ann and Karen and for us—this shared leadership is a welcome reality allowing greater freedom and flexibility. But the idea of letting go in any way can be a tough prospect, particularly for women who have accepted the message that they must be perfect and in complete control at all times.

Deborah Spar explores the pressure women place on themselves to be perfect in everything in *Wonder Women: Sex, Power, and the Quest for Perfection.* "Today," she writes, "women and girls around the world have fallen headlong into this same embrace of blame and failure, into a stubborn pattern of believing that anything less than 'all' in their lives is proof only of their own shortcomings. Rather than acknowledging that feminine perfection is a lie, we continue both to believe in the myth and to feel guilty when we—inevitably, inherently—fall short of it."[27] To work in partnership, women must be willing to give up the quest for control and learn a new way: sharing the load.

Preparing for Risk: A Toolkit

With mutual accountability as the foundation of their collaborations, female partners can do the talking, listening, researching, analyzing, and planning it takes to equip themselves for managing risk when it comes along. Some of the strategies and tools partners use to prepare for risk are pilot projects, partnership agreements, establishing decision-making tactics, and ensuring that communication includes listening as well as talking for both partners. None of these involves rocket science or is specific to women working together—they are just ways of building solid relationships. However, each strategy goes a long way toward developing a healthy collaboration that is strong enough to weather future storms.

Pilot Projects

Pilot projects are those that partners take on before the partnership's official launch to ensure that the collaboration is roadworthy. One of our favorite examples is Valentines Shmalentines, the New York City fundraiser led by Carin Rosenberg

Levine and Julia Lichtman Kepniss, who went on to start Hitched, an upscale bridal salon in Washington, DC. The meticulous planning and organization required for Valentines Shmalentines gave these childhood friends the opportunity to test whether professional partnership was a viable option for them. They decided it was. After being disappointed by the lack of options in bridal stores in Washington when they planned their own weddings, they decided to invest Carin's business background and Julia's law degree in something they both cared about. They opened the doors to Hitched, their bridal salon in 2005 and have been partnering ever since.

Whether your pilot project lasts years, like Julia and Carin's, or is a short-term or one-time trial doesn't matter. What is important is that you and your partner have the chance to test working together and that you take time to frankly assess what worked and what didn't. If honest discussion flows and you are both enthusiastic about pursuing further projects, you'll know you're off to a good start.

Partnership Agreements

In our interviews, we found that some partners had developed official agreements with a lawyer, and others had worked out their own agreements. We recommend doing both. What is most important is that you and your partner take the time alone and together to think and talk through how you will make decisions, resolve conflicts, share profits, invest money, and sell the business. Do this no matter what. Record your conclusions and decisions, and then engage an attorney to make the agreement official.

Christa Granderson-Reid and Janai Nelson, cocreators of the Brownstone Buddies multicultural dolls, held to the maxim "Fail to plan, plan to fail" throughout their start-up. Mothers who met on a playground, formed a friendship, and then started a business, they were determined to develop an agreement that reinforced their new professional relationship. As you shape your agreement, remember to focus as much on potential successes as well as on detours and failures.

Decision-Making Tactics

What will decision-making look like? Who will take the lead? How will follow-up occur? These are questions to be considered as partners determine their tactics.

When Jeanne Sullivan, Deborah Farrington, and Laura Sachar decided to leave their various Wall Street firms to create their own venture-capital entity, StarVest Partners, they took the time early on to determine how best to address decision-making. Working with a consultant, they each took assessment tests, such as the Myers-Briggs Type Indicator® (MBTI®), to gain a sense of their individual styles and the potential strengths and challenges they might face as a group. What they discovered was that they were good at making decisions but liked analytical rigor, which sometimes slowed them down.

Deborah, a former chairman of an executive-staffing

firm with $250 million in revenue, sometimes felt frustrated by the way the process could "slow down to the speed of the slowest person." Discussing these topics early in their partnership created the groundwork for continuing to work on their decision-making process in the following years. Deborah reflected, "There's frustration in partnership, but it's the way to go. We have learned to move decision-making along and still get buy-in at every stage of the process." Ultimately their approach has led to grounded outcomes, furthering the firm's vision, fulfilling its values, and resulting in success. StarVest Partners is the largest woman-majority-owned venture-capital firm in the United States, with $400 million under management.[28]

Clarifying the decision-making process is critically important for the health of your collaboration, because this is where egos can clash and get in the way. If you are someone who always likes to have the final say, ask yourself if you are truly willing to share decision-making. Are you able to listen to and fairly weigh other opinions? And if you tend to nod along to keep the peace, you should recognize the implications: going with the flow and against your grain might damage the outcomes you are working hard to create. We recommend following the lead of the StarVest Partners, taking time in the beginning of your collaboration to assess your decision-making styles and talk through how you will handle conflicting ideas and potential stalemates.

Sometimes, the need for a decision-making structure can emerge in response to a new initiative. Our experience of writing *Power Through Partnership* is one example. When we began writing, we both revised, and edited without any sense of who had the final say. We ended up writing in circles, each of us revising and starting over with every draft. Finally, Maggie threw up her hands and asked Betsy to serve as the lead writer who would make the ultimate decisions when we became caught in a back-and-forth. The new structure clarified the process, allowing us to write and build on each other's ideas in a far more effective way.

Communication: Talking and *Listening*

Tools developed in the early stages of partnership are not meant to be one-time-only fixes. Healthy collaborations require consistent maintenance checks. The partners we talked with confirmed that in the strongest partnerships the practice of talking is well balanced. This means that the partners maintain a steady flow of communication: not too much, not too little, and with equal opportunities for talking and listening for all partners.

A pattern we have observed in many partnerships is that communication gushes in the early stages—there's a lot to talk through and many decisions to be made! But as time passes, the intensity lessens. This isn't a sign of a fading relationship or a stale business model. Rather, it indicates a maturing collaboration that has become more efficient. With clear roles and boundaries and plenty of trust, partners no longer need to check in at every turn: they know they can trust their partner to do what she has committed to do.

Of course, balance is critical. Collaborations can suffer if communication slackens too much and maintenance checks go by the wayside. Claudia, the woman we talked with on the train in San Francisco, whose business had rapidly expanded, is a good example. She and her partner lost their connection with each other as they became wrapped up in the demands of a booming business, and the communication breakdown contributed to the end of their partnership.

An Inventory of Risks

Since our partnership began in 2002, we have weathered plenty of what-ifs, some wonderful, some terrible: one cancer diagnosis and subsequent treatment; one spouse's job loss; four parents' relocations; two parents' hospitalizations; one childbirth; four growing children; workload ups and downs; a monster of a recession; and the flow of new projects and clients. And that's just what comes to mind. Each incident—from the most personal to the purely professional—wove its way into the fabric of collaboration as we figured out how to make room, support each other, and leverage any opportunities that might arrive.

Through all the ups and downs, risks, and in-betweens, our business has grown stronger, and our collaboration has grown surprisingly elastic as we have stretched it in directions we could not have predicted when we imagined possibilities at Maggie's kitchen table.

We want to circle back to the beginning of this chapter

to repeat the wise words shared by ROWE's Jody Thompson, "The greatest risk to partnership is no partnership at all." Over the past twelve years, nothing has been truer for us.

Chapter 6

Leveraging Conflict

Because partners, female or male, make big decisions and take risks together, conflict is inevitable. It's the elephant in the room, ready to wiggle its hairy trunk and flap its big ears between partners. And it's going to occur no matter how hard you try to prevent it from happening. Sometimes conflict rears its head right in the middle of a stressful, busy, crazy situation, where much is at stake and all anyone wants is for it to go away. But it won't. It just stands there smack dab in the middle of everything. It's what you do with it that matters. Because unless the opposing ideas, interests, or needs of the partners are resolved, the uncomfortable emotions and tension caused by the conflict will simmer under the surface, disturbing normal workflow and camaraderie.

Facing Conflict

Most of us recognize that conflict is best faced directly. But for many women (and a fair number of men), the prospect of confronting brewing tensions in a crucial relationship is even more daunting than the prospect of facing a live elephant. However, conflict need not be painful or messy or bitter. Furthermore, the energy generated by conflict can actually be put to good use. In the best circumstances, conflict is a productive force that can strengthen a partnership and create new opportunities for conversation and creativity. Such results, though, can occur only when partners are willing to face and resolve issues together instead of tiptoeing past them.

Our entrepreneurial friend Tanya had just started a partnership with her former college roommate, Denise, when she called Maggie for advice. "What should I do? Denise isn't following up on any of the tasks she promised she'd do to get the business off the ground."

"Have you talked about it?" Maggie asked.

"Well, we talked about what needed to get done, but then she didn't do her part," Tanya answered.

"OK, but did you talk about what's getting in the way?"

Long pause from Tanya and then, "Uhhh, well, she's really busy doing other things and I don't want to bother her with this."

"Sounds like you're really frustrated," Maggie said, stating the obvious.

"I am! It's like Denise doesn't even care."

"What would happen if you talked about what's going on right now before you get more frustrated?"

"I don't want Denise to get mad at me," Tanya sighed.

"So, what would happen if you waited to talk about it?"

A longer pause and then Tanya admitted, "The problem won't go away, will it? I'll just get more upset and then I'll get angrier and then she really will hate me."

Tanya knew she was going to get angrier and yet was willing to do just about anything to avoid talking with Denise, including putting up with an unbalanced partnership. By avoiding the conflict, Tanya was fanning the flames of fear. Why? Tanya was afraid the conflict could upset an early working relationship, terrified Denise would see her as uptight or demanding—or worse—and scared that Denise would bolt. Instead of talking with Denise about the assumptions she was making, Tanya was treading lightly, trying not to make waves, and building resentment—her own and possibly Denise's as well—with every frustrated moment. She knew what had to be done but she didn't want to do it, even though avoiding it was upping the already hot temperature.

Yet the risks of not talking are far greater. Misunderstandings, negative emotions, tensions, anxieties, and fears will grow until something blows up. Failed schedules, broken promises, botched projects, and even failure of the partnership can be the fallout.

What might happen if, rather than evading the conflict and allowing her resentment to fester, Tanya approached Denise and checked in? Maybe Denise would get angry; maybe Tanya would as well. But would that be any more difficult than what Tanya was doing? Maybe Denise would share her own assumptions, opening the way to an honest discussion about the dynamics that weren't working in their partnership.

Of course the operative word in all these possible scenarios is *maybe*. But if they begin talking, they might at least discover an opening that could lead to resolution. By being open and willing to wade into uncertain conversations, partners can move forward and find workable solutions, strengthening their collaboration and paving the way for productive discussions in the future. Of course this is easier said than done for women who have been raised to avoid open conflict and to handle it under the radar instead, as we explored in Chapter 3.

In our interviews, partners shared stories about how they have moved past the threatening aspects of confrontation as they learned to channel the energy from a disagreement into a professional outlet. One illustration comes from Savannah's Chroma Gallery co-owners, artists Lori Keith Robinson and Jan Clayton-Pagratis. Lori and Jan were overworked and exhausted when their first argument erupted. As tempers began to flare, Lori found herself cranking up Motown music, and she and Jan stopped fighting and began painting. Sharing the same canvas, each brushstroke built on the next as Lori and Jan collaborated on what would become their first "Loja" (a combination of the artists' names). Rechanneling their energy into art calmed the mood and allowed a resolution to emerge. In addition, this series of vibrant abstract paintings now symbolizes the partnership and sets Chroma apart, attracting new customers and sales. Both the collaborative painting process and its results are tangible reflections of the partners' ability to use conflict as a source for creativity.

Across the board, women partners say that they have too much to accomplish to waste time in unproductive, meaningless skirmishes that result from stewing or basking in resentment. Jennifer, Ursula, Maria, Gabrielle, and Charity Burton, real-life sisters who together form the Five Sisters Production Company, told us their conflicts are productive because of the respect at the core of their multifaceted collaboration. As Maria shared with us, "We can have conflict and at times it's heated, but there's a safety in knowing that we will all work it out and we give each other the freedom to express ourselves and the space to work it through."

Sometimes working through the conflict to get what needs to be done is less about freedom and more about have-to. The award-winning movie *Dallas Buyers Club* had already experienced more than its share of ups and downs when investors backed out ten weeks before filming. Producer Rachel Winter "was feeding the crew, which had arrived in New Orleans for preproduction, with her personal credit cards." As her female coproducer, Robbie Brenner, described it on NPR, "We just willed that movie into existence.… We willed it. We willed it. *We willed it.* There was no time to … pull out our hair and yell and scream. We did what women do best, which is just deal."[29] If "just dealing" is something a woman does best, imagine the added impact of bringing together two or more female partners who know not only how to manage stressful situations but also how to collaborate to achieve results.

A Case for True Kindness

As partners successfully deal together with conflict, the confidence between them expands, trust increases, commitment grows, and an authentic kindness emerges. By *true kindness* we mean the honesty and directness to say what needs to be said, even if it is hard to say and difficult for the other person to hear. We contrast this type of honest kindness to the sugarcoated politeness, or niceness, women have been raised to express.

The authenticity of true kindness must be intentionally cultivated by partners. Even Lauren Parkesian and Molly Thompson, the cocreators of the KIND Campaign, a national program that teaches middle-school girls to care for instead of bully each other, had to figure out how to balance honest directness and kindness in their own communication. As Molly described, "In the beginning, there were certain things that needed to be talked about and we were still learning how to express ourselves without jeopardizing our friendship and the business. It was important for us to learn to say, 'I don't feel great about this and let's talk about it.' We made it harder on ourselves because we didn't know how to say things to each other so we would hold onto it for a couple of weeks before saying it. As females we are taught to be sweet and to be nice so we don't know how to have a confrontation."

Learning how to engage in direct, honest conversation is an important developmental step for partners as they move from the "nice-girl" conditioning to what it means to be genuinely kind. Sometimes women assume that if they just say nice things and speak in pleasant voices about other women, they are being kind. This is what North Carolinians like us call the "bless-her-heart" syndrome. The phrase gives women license to say whatever they want about someone else, no matter how disparaging it is, as long as "bless her heart" is added to the end of the remark.

But kindness and that sort of politeness couldn't be more different. Kindness is an outgrowth of trust and compassion, whereas politeness is a conflict-avoidance tactic drilled into us since girlhood. Kindness is a connector, a way to genuinely lessen conflict, whereas politeness is a shield women use to deflect conflict. By being polite, we actually create unproductive conflict by diluting the meaning of our messages. Kindness is a direct interest in someone else's welfare; politeness is a protection of one's own welfare. When women are in collaboration, kindness means everything, whereas politeness masks conflict while simultaneously stirring it.

Nicola Kraus, co-author of *The Nanny Diaries*, beautifully summed up the dangers of being too polite. In our interview, her advice to women considering partnership was, "Be prepared. This is a business, a professional endeavor. Be considerate but don't be too polite or you won't get anything accomplished. You're responsible for that person and there are times when you're going to give up something that you thought you never would. Be prepared for that." Co-author Emma McLaughlin weighed in, "It's a learning process. In our experience, setting ground rules isn't the first thing a woman does in any situation. We had to find our way through that."

Without the veneer of politeness, it's easier for partners to develop ground rules that guide their work together: setting boundaries, clarifying roles, and identifying responsibilities. Unlike the rules of our girlhoods, which suppress conflict, these ground rules can leverage conflict by giving partners the opportunity to talk through and come to terms with how they want to work together. Betsy recently consulted on a project with our esteemed colleague, Peg Carlson. While, the first half of the project went relatively well, Peg and Betsy reached a point when their own different consulting styles hindered their collaboration. Rather than burying the bubbling conflict, they talked it through. Both recognized that Peg's thoughtful approach and Betsy's quick energy were complementary strengths that could benefit the project instead of interfering with it. But they needed to implement some new ways of working. Their decision to set ground rules, which built in frequent check-ins between them and outlined specific rather than overlapping consulting roles, resulted in a project that achieved the client's desired outcomes and bolstered Peg and Betsy's collaboration.

Eight Strategies for Addressing Conflict

For women who are conditioned to steer clear of conflict, the reframing we're suggesting will take time and practice, even in the safety zone of partnership. Addressing conflict is more challenging than letting it go and figuring things will work themselves out. Sometimes they do, but more often they don't. Deciding whether and when to address conflict is a judgment call. If a relationship matters and isn't going away, as in the Peg and Betsy story, then facing conflict as it arises will benefit the collaboration. Yes, it might be awkward and uncomfortable until you get used to it. But once you're talking it through, the discomfort is likely to fade. Plus the more you do it, the easier it gets. Here are some tips for moving past the fear and dealing with conflict:

1. Remember why you are doing this: to make working together easier.

2. Focus on specific aspects of the conflict rather than on general annoyances. Saying "It really bothered me when you contradicted me during the presentation" is more helpful than "You really bugged me yesterday."

3. Stick with the conflict in hand, avoiding comments that begin, "You always …"

4. Share what you have to say and then listen.

5. Restate what you have heard, "So, what you're saying is …?" This allows you to make sure you understand the other person and gives the person room to modify what she has said.

6. Be prepared to give and accept an honest apology.

7. Once the conflict is resolved, let it go—there's no sense rehashing.

8. Engage the other person in taking the next steps. For instance, how can you take this experience and develop ground rules and strategies that will be useful in future interactions?

We would love to tell you that we woke up one day and—voila!—knew just how to navigate these eight steps, that we've always known how to be the kind of partners who could use conflict productively in kind, confidence-inspiring ways. But that would be a lie. We're as human as you are, girls who grew into women who are prone to tiptoeing, "bless-her-hearting," and doing more than a little tap dancing. The plain truth is that when we address conflict with someone outside our partnership, we still get butterflies. However, partnership has provided a zone where we can talk through tough situations honestly. And with each conversation, our conflict-resolution skills improve.

The-Push-Pull and Other Dynamics

To use conflict in ways that moved our collaboration forward, we've had to recognize a dynamic between us, a push-pull tension that we've since observed in other co-leaderships. In other words, one partner is the "push," the forward mover, the idea generator, whereas the other partner is the "pull," the ballast, the reality checker. This dynamic brings the power to contribute to and to detract from collaborations in equal measure.

In our case, Betsy was usually the push, throwing out new ideas, some wilder than others, to keep the business growing to the next level. Maggie was the pull, preferring to be cautious about taking on new projects that might disrupt whatever precarious balance was already in place. That worked until situations arose in which Betsy pushed against Maggie's pull, leading to a war of wills. Maggie's immediate reaction to Betsy in those situations was most often, "Uh-huh, here she goes again, spinning crazy ideas." And Betsy would think, "Why is Maggie being such a stick-in-the-mud?" We reached the point where we didn't even need to hear what the ideas or the resistances were: we immediately closed our minds to what was being said and replaced each other's words with our own assumptions.

Thanks to our friends Maryanne Perrin and Kella Hatcher, co-founders of Balancing Professionals, a job-placement firm that connected part-time workers to professional positions, who described the role of this tension in their own collaboration, we were able to understand and begin to make the most of the dynamic that was playing out between us. "We had respect for each other from the get-go," Kella told us. "Maryanne is push and I'm pull. That brings us back to the middle." Maryanne added, "We recognize this and talk about it."

We've come to realize that even in the toughest tug-of-wars, we both want what's best for Mulberry and for each other. So instead of getting stuck in a struggle, we now stop and allow ourselves room to name whatever we were pushing or pulling for. For example, when we began the final revision of *Power Through Partnership*, Betsy was feeling stressed by the looming deadline and Maggie was wrapping up other commitments. As we sat down to get our ducks in a row, Betsy said, "With you stressed and me exhausted, we're susceptible to the push-pull. Let's tread lightly."

This labeling provided a chance for both of us to question our assumptions before they were fully baked. Based on all we've learned over the years, we could navigate a tense situation without making it worse. Now that we recognize and understand our push-pull tendency, we are surprised to see that instead of resisting it, we actively leverage it, and sometimes—intentionally or not—we find ourselves switching roles, with Maggie pushing a new idea and Betsy pulling back and keeping things real.

In addition to push-pull dynamics, ordinary human issues such as exhaustion, difficult days, sickness, and feeling overwhelmed by work and life are all potential conflict igniters. Knowing your own and your partner's usual approach to conflict will help you separate the real issue from whatever is clouding it. To identify your typical response, imagine the stickiest situation you can come up with. Maybe resentment is building because your priorities have shifted. Or perhaps she has been on vacation in Tahiti while you've been holding down the fort. Whatever the situation is, what are you most likely to do? (Feel free to add to the list.)

Avoid? Duck and hide—talk about anything but the issue.

Escape? Run for the nearest exit.

Gloss? Smile with your jaw clenched and say "everything's fine" each time your partner tries to discuss the situation.

Air dirty laundry? Discuss this situation with everyone *but* your partner.

Dump? Just let it rip in person, via e-mail, or in a long voice mail in which you say exactly what you think without giving your partner a chance to respond.

Address? Take a deep breath, then discuss the issue thoroughly.

All of these are routine human responses to conflict. And knowing which ones you're more likely to use, especially when you're not on your game, will help you stay honest and clear about the actual conflict and what's blocking you from facing it. Fortunately, this critical partnership skill will improve and grow easier with practice. You will learn to check in with each other to prevent some conflicts from arising. And you will discover that sometimes it's better to let go. With practice, this, too, will become easier. Ultimately, learning to address conflict will not only strengthen your partnership but will also foster personal growth.

In summary, there's no room for girlhood rules in healthy partnerships. We've learned through our own partnership that conflict and its feisty cousin, competition, need not be covert. In fact, everyone involved is better off when conflicts are out in the open. Productive conflict produces energy, opportunities for looking at things differently, and chances to move forward in more meaningful ways.

Blockages and Other Difficulties

Of course, some conflicts are tougher to step back from and reframe than others. Sometimes enormous fear may surround the conflict, perhaps because the partnership is newer and more fragile. Or the conflict might be just one in a tangle of many tensions (although unraveling one could lead to the heart of the conflict, a potentially productive notion). Often conflict becomes bogged down because partners' values and goals are not aligned, making it hard or impossible for partners to see eye to eye because their hearts are in different places. Another blockage point might be a clash of egos, a sign of a collaboration that's not yet aligned, requiring an investment of time, trust, and commitment from all partners to overcome.

We have also seen that as partners move into different life phases, priorities shift, assumptions can change, and expectations can collide. For women, who often bear the brunt of childrearing and elder care, life transitions can arouse conflicts between partners that once seemed settled. An interview with partners who had contentedly worked at the same pace until a new baby entered the picture showed the stresses a major life change can cause for partnership. Plans for Jane and Eliza's event-planning company seemed tight but abruptly halted when Eliza was unable to find adequate care for her new baby. Jane, who didn't have children, wanted and needed Eliza to continue co-leading the business. Eliza was weighed down by the stress of figuring out child care while balancing a heavy load of guilt over the tough choice between letting down Jane or not being as available to her baby and growing family. After a few frustrating months, Eliza left the partnership.

Assumptions and expectations underlie these impasses. Perhaps with honest conversation and reexamination of partners' priorities, the partnership could have survived, but at the time no other choice seemed possible. This is another incidence where role models could have helped the partners think about their situation differently. If only Eliza and Jane had known Nancy Duff Campbell and Marcia Greenberger from National Women's Law Center, who have worked together as co-leaders since 1978. Over their decades-long collaboration, Nancy and Marcia have experienced many phases of partnership and could have advised Eliza and Jane of the ebb and flow to come through the years. Nancy's and Marcia's wisdom about the life cycle of their own partnership could have added valuable perspective. They could have shared stories about how they managed maternity leaves, how they maintained balance when their children were little, and how they flexed their schedules when needed.

As Eliza and Jane moved past the phase of caring for young children, Nancy and Marcia could have advised them about how to sustain their partnership, how to manage successes, and how to allow the ongoing flexibility needed to make room for short-term leaves for unexpected illnesses and extended leaves for long-deserved vacations. Most of all, what these mentors could have shared is that sometimes taking the long view can make all the difference in the way you approach solving problems.

Taking the Long View

Nancy and Marcia and the many others, regardless of gender, who are traveling the partnership road can confirm that conflict along the way is inevitable but not fatal. What matters is how partners handle and resolve conflicts. So, the next time that big lumbering elephant called conflict marches into your collaboration, you can turn away and ignore it while it grows bigger or you can invite it to sit down so you and your partner can take a frank look. Talk it through, like Molly and Lauren of the Kind Campaign. Trust that the elephant will grow tamer over time. And when you can, take the long view of the whole majestic beauty of that creature instead of just the parts that are getting in the way.

Once you become more comfortable with conflict, like the painters Lori and Jan, you can put it to work for your partnership. Use its energy to create art, develop plans, generate ideas, build new products, and imagine possibilities. When you use conflict to crack open your assumptions and peer into someone else's, you are learning what makes you and your partner tick. Allowing conflict and using it productively with a trusted partner will change you as well as your collaboration. The courage to name what you see and take responsibility for your own stuff is just one of the gifts conflict can bring.

The Rubber Band Theory

People love happy endings. We go to the movies so we can feel at peace when the story ends on a high note. We walk out of the theater and back into our lives, imagining the characters staying just as they were on screen, wide smiles frozen in perpetuity—at least until the sequel.

If we were making the movie of our partnership, the ideal happy ending would have been when Maggie's leukemia went into remission and our partnership grew stronger because we faced these challenging times together. As in a Bollywood film, the credits would have rolled over plenty of dancing and singing and celebrating.

But because this is real life, that's not what happened. Instead, Maggie's diagnosis and treatment were important steps in the trajectory of our long and winding collaboration, but nothing close to its grand finale. Our partnership has marched on since then, as we keep adapting and stretching, celebrating the ups and making our way through the downs. Life rarely, if ever, moves in a neat progression that culminates in a crashing crescendo. And as we explore in this chapter, neither do partnerships.

The Transitions of Partnership

Our interviews with partners revealed that partnerships typically experience many transitions during their lifetimes. By transitions we mean any change that alters the path of the partnership, such as a shift in leadership, direction, structure, or priorities. Such transitions are part of the life cycle of a partnership as it grows and matures. Whether the shifts are externally or internally driven; positive, negative, or neutral in effect; subtle or overwhelming doesn't seem to matter. What we learned is that partnerships based on trust, mutual accountability, and flexibility can survive periods of upheaval. They can grow, bend, stretch, and reshape themselves—and in the best cases they return to the center stronger than before.

The Rubber Band Theory

The good news is that women's collaborations are usually much more durable than the myths from Chapter 3 might indicate. As co-leaders reorganize in response to change, they find that their collaborations develop a kind of give and stretch as trust between partners matures. This is the rubber band theory of partnership. To demonstrate, place a rubber band around your wrist. Pull the band away from your wrist. Hold it. Stretch it as far as it can stretch. Now let the rubber band snap back.

(Careful: it's not our goal to inflict pain.)

This stretch and snap back to center is a quality we've observed in healthy collaborations that gives partners the space to discover new ways of working beyond the boundaries of the collaboration. The change might mean exploring new separate opportunities or beginning to collaborate with other partners. The extent of the stretch varies, depending on the situation, and where partners are in the life cycle of their collaboration. (We can't help noting that this is yet another departure from the marriage metaphor, in which seeing other people takes on a whole new meaning.)

The rubber band theory was inspired by the experiences of *Legally Blonde* screenwriters Kiwi Smith and Karen McCullah, partners for whom stretching has meant gaining wider perspectives from working apart sometimes, either solo or by teaming up with other collaborators. Their ventures away from screenwriting have included producing movies, writing poetry, and writing novels for young adults. Kiwi told us that the independent projects she and Karen have undertaken "made possible our longevity as a partnership because we were able to have the freedom to do our own stuff."

Karen was quick to point out the pros and cons of solo work, "You're not bound to others' opinions, but the downside is you're not getting opinions either." Yet both Kiwi and Karen know where they can find opinions: back in their own partnership, to which they keep on returning, with renewed appreciation for the seamlessness, efficiency, honest perspectives, and joy it provides.

Returning to one's partnership with increasing appreciation is what gives elasticity its value. Partners aren't just stretching out, away from and beyond partnership, but are coming back to its core, enhancing their collaborations with the new perspectives, skills, understanding, and funny stories gleaned "out there." And what do partners take to these new opportunities? The skills and experience they have developed through their partnerships!

Singer-songwriters Amy Ray and Emily Saliers of the Indigo Girls have been stretching their partnership for decades, finding that the partnership directly benefits when each partner pursues separate projects. As Emily said in our interview, "We're both happy to have productive individual lives separate from each other. We're happy when things happen to us individually, and we're happy when things happen to us as the Indigo Girls. It's a very functional relationship."

Amy and Emily's identities blend together like their harmonies, at least for the thousands of fans who have followed them for decades. Understanding that this sort of fusion is inevitable, each has worked to carve out her own independent persona and pursuits. "There are moments when you need your own creative space," Amy said. "Emily is writing books with her dad, and she has her own restaurant. If we need validation [for us as individuals], we get it outside the partnership."

We understand. Each of us has been confused for the other. We were even called "Metsy" by one client, who said with a chuckle, "It's just easier to think of you as one person."

These fused identities can grow tiring, of course, making opportunities for a little separation now and again all the more appealing. Yet they are also testaments to the power of the entity that partners develop together. We find it gratifying when our clients think of us as Mulberry, the consulting practice we worked so hard to build. This balance the rubber band theory provides—between the power of the entity and the opportunity to stretch as individuals—is one of the many gifts of partnership.

For Tina Kuna and Stephanie Allen, the co-founders of Dream Dinners, elasticity has meant expanding their long-held leadership roles. When we met with the partners for lunch in the tavern near Dream Dinners' Snohomish, Washington, headquarters, the pair was exploring the possibility of Stephanie pursuing new media opportunities to promote the company's brand while Tina continued to run the company from Snohomish. Even as they were reconsidering the way in which they structured their roles, each was clear that these changes would not occur unless they were both willing and open to them. Stephanie said, "The truth always floats to the top. If one of us isn't ready, we'll put it aside for a while, and wait until we both feel it's really the right thing." Tina filled in the other side of the story—that even if one partner wasn't quite ready for the change, "I don't think either of us would want to deny the other one what's truly in her heart." That sense of mutual respect and reciprocity has kept their partnership going.

What It Takes to Stretch

The Dream Dinners story exemplifies the qualities needed for a partnership to stretch without snapping. Mutual respect and trust must be well established so that each partner believes without question that her partner's intentions are good. Mutual accountability becomes even more important as partners communicate from a distance. As collaborations expand, partners must be mindful not to shift into autopilot mode when it comes to the communication and commitment they may have long taken for granted.

As we discussed in Chapter 5's exploration of risks, partners need not be in constant contact, nor should they be. But they do need reliable access and the comfort of knowing they can count on responsiveness from their partners. Relationships matter—these are women in partnership, after all. And elastic partnerships require even more relationship maintenance than static collaborations do. Vigilant interaction and firm commitment to the partnership can allow the give without the snap.

The Elasticity Path

Like many partnerships, ours took years to mature into elasticity. Eight years ago, we wouldn't have considered pursuing separate paths. We entertained the idea of new opportunities but never separately; we considered the possibility of working with other partners but couldn't imagine working with anyone else as seamlessly as we collaborated together.

Our perceptions have evolved since then because of the knowledge gleaned from other partners. These role models helped us see that by allowing our individual needs to stretch, we could strengthen rather than weaken our partnership. The freedom to stretch would be a sign of the durable elasticity of our own collaboration. By following in other partners' footsteps, we have been able to expand to allow room for Betsy to take on new consulting projects and enlarge her individual coaching practice and for Maggie to pursue a second graduate degree and opportunities in the field of education. In doing so, we've enhanced our partnership and the relationship at its core by weaving together our new learnings, sharing our perspectives, and turning to each other for guidance and laughter as we make sense of our new terrains. We still depend on each other for perspective, reality checking, and support, and we cherish the freedom to be ourselves with each other more than ever.

With the extra attention we pay to maintaining trust, communication, and commitment, the emerging divergent directions we once thought were a risk to partnership are actually just the opposite. Whereas once upon a time our partnership might have gotten stuck when we couldn't foresee how independent projects worked within it, now we understand and embrace the fact that we'll figure it out as we always do— by trusting each other and frequently checking in.

Handling Inevitable Endings with Grace

Of course, even the toughest rubber band can only stretch so far. Because our interviews with partners have spanned several years, it isn't a big surprise to find that some have dissolved. After all, life happens, extenuating situations occur, relationships fade, priorities shift, businesses change, and partnerships end. What is surprising is that conflict was not the reason for most of these dissolutions. In contrast to myths spun about women in co-leadership positions, these stories included no catfights, no name-calling, no explosions—none of the drama long associated with women dealing with ruptured relationships. Instead, many of the partners we talked with highlighted the effort they took to end their partnership as respectfully and with as much integrity as they started it. What these partners had in common was their willingness to face an ending as part of the partnership by laying the relational groundwork that prepared partners far in advance of the actual conclusion.

For Amy and Emily of the Indigo Girls, the room to stretch has become a standard operating feature in their long-time collaboration. However, for Jennifer Niesslein and Stephanie Wilkinson, the co-founders of *Brain, Child: The Magazine for Thinking Mothers,* elasticity helped prepare for the ending that came years later.

When we first interviewed Jennifer and Stephanie, who met as young mothers in need of a literary fix and went on to create the kind of magazine they wanted to read, they were testing the elasticity of their seven-year collaboration. While

Chapter 7: The Rubber Band Theory

Stephanie operated the magazine in Lexington, Virginia, Jennifer was at home in Charlottesville writing her first book, *Practically Perfect in Every Way: My Journey Though the World of Self-Help*. As a result of their flexibility, Jennifer was able to pursue a long-time dream of writing a book. Stephanie pursued a dream of her own a couple of years later when she opened the Red Hen, Lexington's first farm-to-fork restaurant.

When we followed up six years later, Jennifer and Stephanie had recently sold their thirteen-year-old, highly respected magazine to a fan and were pursuing separate ventures. Stephanie shared the emotional impact this transaction had on both founders, "This was something we worked so hard to build and then to sell. It is a testament to our relationship that I'm completely content with the outcome." The pair remain good friends who continue to be open to and excited about future collaborations.

Kristi Hedges and Elizabeth Shea, co-founders of the Washington, DC, technology-marketing firm SheaHedges, also intentionally dissolved their partnership with their mutual respect and integrity intact. When Kristi decided to sell her stake in the business to Elizabeth, the pair worked with a mediator and an attorney to ensure they were both comfortable with the transition from shared to solo leadership. The transitioning partners decided not to speak publicly about the change for three months, allowing time to present a united front to employees and clients. Elizabeth and Kristi's graceful, intentional exit left the entity, which continues today under the name SpeakerBox Communications, in good stead. And like Stephanie and Jennifer, they paved the way for the future collaborations, which have since occurred between the partners.

The reality of an inevitable ending was a constant presence in the partnership of Isabel Yuriko Stenzel Byrnes and Anabel Mariko Stenzel, identical twins, co-authors, and creative partners who lived under the cloud of cystic fibrosis and all its complications until Anabel died in 2013. The sisters were powered by partnership as they encouraged each other to achieve incredible goals: beating the odds against a chronic and deadly disease, swimming and running competitively, enduring multiple lung transplants, cowriting their memoir, *The Power of Two: A Twin Triumph Over Cystic Fibrosis,* and taking part in the production of a subsequent documentary, all while pursuing their own relationships and independent careers (social work for Anabel and genetic and grief counseling for Isabel).

After Anabel died, Isabel wrote us to say, "I'm thankful for the forty-one years Anabel and I shared and the tools that have helped me deal with this significant loss." What kinds of tools, we wondered, could possibly prepare someone, let alone a sister and a twin, for the end of a four-decade collaboration? Isabel elaborated, "It's a simple message. When our realtor sold us our house, he told us that the best time to prepare for resale is when you buy the house. The same is true for partnership. As business partners, you have to prepare to end when you start." Courageously facing each stage of a partnership with the end in mind allows partners to prepare for graceful exits. And as Anabel and Isabel's story so clearly reinforces, it allows partners to richly savor the time they spend together.

Nobody said ending a partnership (or beginning it or keeping it going, for that matter) would be a walk in the park. Facing the idea, let alone the reality, of an ending isn't easy. Doing so requires partners to be honest about the possibility that something unknown could happen to the partnership, to the business, or to the partners themselves. But these partners have found ways to honorably and respectfully make their way through the many green lights, detours, yields, and stop signs on the road through partnership.

The Greatest Resource

As partners shift gears, hold on, let go, move forward, flex, or stay in step, their most vibrant resource is the relationship at the core of their collaborations. With care, these central relationships will continue and flourish long after the partnership has run its course. Fear of the bitter cost of ruined relationships might prevent some women from joining forces, but the promise and reality of rich, interwoven partnerships inspires brave, bold women to do all they can to form and preserve such relationships from the very beginning to long after the inevitable end.

It's this relationship—based on trust, honesty, and respect, and offering freedom, confidence, joy, and shared accountability—that sticks with female partners. What often emerges from these healthy collaborations is the enduring ability of partners to tap into each other as resources, sometimes long after the collaboration has ended. Screenwriter Kiwi Smith joked with her cowriter Karen McCullah Lutz that Karen probably had a little sign on her desk saying, "What would Kiwi say?" for those times when they weren't working closely together. We wonder if many partners carry this mental reminder: what would she do?

Stretching the Rubber Band

What will be the greatest gift of your partnership? Will it be the trust-based, honest, respectful, mutually accountable relationship you and your partner have worked hard to build? Perhaps it will be the confidence you inspire in each other? Maybe it will be the freedom from having to apologize for or cover up how you really feel with a partner who gets it and gets you. It might be the results you achieve and the values you fulfill. Or, with all these pieces in place, will it be the opportunities that arrive when you and your partner stretch your collaboration in exciting new directions, knowing you will return to a core that strengthens as your partnership grows? These are gifts of partnership. More than that, they are the outcomes of a leadership solution for women who are ready for better ways to gain equity on an inequitable landscape.

Moving Forward

Look at you: you're ready for the benefits partnership brings! You have debunked the myths, are equipped to face conflict, and are ready to plunge into the risk of forming a partnership that will stretch and grow with you. You've got what it takes to build a healthy, successful, and sane collaboration of your own. As you move forward, keep on checking in. Build in regular times to stop and assess the state of your working relationship. Ensure that trust is alive and well. Make sure that the results you accomplish fulfill the values that matter to both of you and achieve the benefits of partnership. Recalibrate as needed. Stretch that collaboration and give it room to return to center.

A Call to Action

Partnership works too well for women to remain lost under the radar. Help spread the word about the power that comes through partnership to all the women you know who are searching for better ways to work and lead. You can do this by:

- Shining the spotlight on partner role models. Other women can learn from the lessons and stories of these co-leaders, as we have through our interviews and you have in your reading. The partners featured in this book aren't the only ones out there, of course. Instead of stumbling upon them or searching high and low to find them, let's make the female collaborations as visible as those of their male counterparts.

- Shoving aside the myths that obscure the path to partnership. As we have discovered, they are constructed more of history and fable than of reality.

- Spreading the word. Men have *bromance*—defined as a close, nonromantic relationship between two or more men[30]—and women need a word of their own for these relationships that are complex, dynamic, and powerful. We suggest *sistership*, and without further ado, we encourage you to get out there, start a sistership of your own, and spread the word about its powerful benefits.

While you are off building your partnership—your sistership—we hope you will maximize its flexibility and shape it to your own design. Take full advantage of all the benefits of partnership: the freedom to be yourself, the incredible support, the confidence, the equity and power that can result through it, and the ability to operationalize big goals, knowing there are at least two accountable partners to keep track and do the work.

These are our partnership wishes for you: go forth, partner, and celebrate the successes you achieve along the path of this better way to work and lead together.

Notes

1.   Stephanie Coontz, "Why Gender Equity Stalled," *New York Times,* February 16, 2013.

2.   Anne-Marie Slaughter, "Why Women Still Can't Have It All," *The Atlantic,* July/August, 2012.

3.   http://www.catalyst.org/knowledge/women-ceos-and-heads-financial-post-500.

4.   http://www.catalyst.org/regions/united-states.

5.   Frank Bruni, "Women's Unequal Lot," *New York Times,* http://www.nytimes.com/2014/04/13/opinion/sunday/bruni-womens-unequal-lot.html? r=0.

6.   http://www.firstpost.com/photos/twitter-ipo-at-new-york-stock-exchange-1218077.html.

7.   Brigid Schulte, *Overwhelmed: Work, Love, and Play When No One Has the Time* (New York: Farrar, Straus and Giroux, Sarah Crichton Books, 2014), 77.

8.   *National Alliance for Caregiving and AARP, Caregiving in the U.S. (Washington, DC: National Alliance for Caregiving,* 2009; updated November 2012; https://caregiver.org/selected-caregiver-statistics.

9.   http://www.aarp.org/content/dam/aarp/research/public_policy_institute/econ_sec/2013/uphill-climb-women-face-greater-obstacles-retirement-security-AARP-ppi-econ-sec.pdf.

10. Pauline R. Clance and Suzanne A. Imes, "The impostor phenomenon in high achieving women: Dynamics and therapeutic intervention," *Psychotherapy: Theory, Research, and Practice* (1978).

11. Katty Kay and Claire Shipman, *The Confidence Code: The Science and Art of Self-Assurance: What Women Should Know* (New York: HarperCollins, 2014), xv.

12. http://thedailyshow.cc.com/videos/snggjc/the-broads-must-be-crazy.

13. Deborah Tannen, *You Just Don't Understand* (New York: Ballantine Books, 1990), 25.

14. Louann Brizendine, *The Female Brain* (New York: Broadway Books, 2006), 8.

15. Tannen, *You Just Don't Understand*, 25.

16. John Gerzema and Michael D'Antonio, *The Athena Doctrine: How Women (and the Men Who Think Like Them) Will Rule the Future* (San Francisco: Jossey-Bass, 2013).

17. Stephanie Coontz, "Why Gender Equity Stalled," *New York Times*, February 16, 2013.

18. Chad Brooks, http://www.huffingtonpost.com/2014/04/09/business-partnerships-women-study_n_5117809.html, published April 8, 2014.

19. Helen Fielding, *Bridget Jones: Mad About the Boy* (New York: Knopf, 2013), 291.

20. Rachel Simmons, *Odd Girl Out: The Hidden of Aggression in Girls* (Orlando, FL: Harcourt, 2002), 22.

21. Audrey Nelson, "From Playground to Battleground: Where Women and Men Learn Conflict Styles and Gender Differences," in *He Speaks, She Speaks*, www.psychologytoday.com, April 25, 2012.

22. Sheryl Sandberg, *Lean In: Women, Work, and the Will to Lead* (New York: Knopf, 2013), 163.

23. Sandberg, *Lean In*, 162.

24. http://www.ak-env.com/home/holder/awards, accessed March 15, 2014.

25.   Sandberg, *Lean In,* 93.

26.   William Sertl, *Life Reimagined,* "Inside Ann Patchett's Bookstore," http://lifereimagined.aarp.org/stories/5591-Inside-Ann-Patchett-s-Bookstore, January 31, 2014

27.   Deborah Spar, *Wonder Women: Sex, Power, and the Quest for Perfection* (New York: Farrar, Straus and Giroux, Sarah Crichton Books, 2013), 29.

28.   http://www.starvestpartners.com/assets/Uploads /StarVest-Fact-Sheet-2014.pdf.

29.   Neda Ulaby, "Morning Edition," *National Public Radio,* February 18, 2014.

30.   Wikipedia.org/wiki/Bromance.

Acknowledgments

We gratefully acknowledge:

Cindi Liston, our third partner and cherished long-time friend, who cheerfully reviewed and critiqued multiple drafts and brought iced coffee when we needed it most.

Anne-Marie Slaughter for saying yes and writing the foreword.

Gary Friedlander for his generosity and immense kindness.

Eric Bates, who shared astute feedback on our early proposals and graciously responded to every "Hey, do you know …?" e-mail.

Peter Guzzardi for the breakfasts and guidance—the Prius is coming.

Lisa Volk for providing support, both administrative and moral.

Christina Baker Kline, who took time from her own busy writing schedule to read an early draft and give feedback.

Mike Smith for the sustained support and friendship. We have a great role for you in the movie.

Peg Carlson for being a valued mentor and trusted colleague.

Rachel Seidman for making the connections.

Margaret Heffernan for taking our story giant leaps ahead.

Amy Tiemann for helping us to figure out our way through this wide, wide world of book writing. And the members of the Advisory Circle for passionately reminding us of the real meaning of sanity when it comes to women's lives.

Acknowledgments

Barry Yeoman for encouraging us to trust our own story.

Chris Allen for being there when we needed you.

Sue Egnoto and Jeff Cohen for sharing your marketing savvy.

Diane Umstead for being a great partner, and the folks at the North Carolina Partnership for Children, for your flexibility, patience, and encouragement.

Nancy Martin, Susan Cohen, Emily Young, and Heidi Tyson for putting us on your radars.

Susan Prager Banner, Joanna Strober, Lauren Whitehurst, Nancy Peacock, Jessica Thomas, Susan Davis, Andrew Park, Tony Brown, and Mari Lazar for being advocates and allies.

Matt Springer, Heather Benjamin, and Tom Volk for invaluable legal guidance.

Jamie Fiocco and Sally Stollmack for making Flyleaf Books the special place that it is: where else can one get mental sustenance, expert guidance, and fabulous jewelry under one roof?

Carolyn Kepcher, Harleen Kahlon, and Kendall Allen for helping us build a platform, brick by brick.

Adrianne Gibilisco, Danielle Goodman, and Nancy Dekkar for the thorough and insightful reviews.

BK authors *Jeannie Coyle, Wendy Axelrod, Diana Whitney and Marcia Reynolds* for guiding our way.

The Weymouth Center for Arts and the Humanities for providing us with much-needed space where we could just write.

And our hard-working interns through the years: *Sharon Schulze, Jane Herzeca, Sarah Jane Maxted, Katie Alberts, Will Connor, Sarah Shapiro, and Holly Lance.*

This book wouldn't have come into existence if . . .

Betsy hadn't taken a chance at Pitchapalooza and connected with the Book Doctors *David Henry Sterry* and *Arielle Eckstut,* who in turn linked us with our agent extraordinaire, *Herb Schaffner* of Big Fish Media.

Acknowledgments

Thank you, Herb, for seeing what could be, answering a thousand questions with kindness and knowledge, and for ultimately getting our proposal in the hands of the amazing team at Berrett-Koehler Publishers: *Kristen Frantz, Katie Sheehan, Kat Engh, Dianne Platner, Courtney Schonfeld, Michael Crowley, and Steve Piersanti.* We are especially grateful to our editors, *Jeevan Sivasubramaniam, Anna Leinberger,* and *Charlotte Ashlock,* for the steadfast guidance and the inspiration to help us to face the big question: Why partnership works for women now?

Finally, thanks to the family and many friends who have loved and supported us, never once asking (at least not out loud), is this really ever going to happen?

From Betsy, thank you to:

My parents, *Ollie and Sam Polk,* for trusting, loving, and believing in me, and for never, ever clipping my wings.

My very first partner, my sister, *Nancy Friedlander.*

Pauline, Rod, and all the *Josephs, Dunlaps, Dubows,* and *Kipas* for letting me know how deeply you care.

Marc for never doubting, and ceaselessly encouraging, for unquestioned love, and unconditional support—I am so lucky to travel this road with you!

Michael, whose open kindness, curiosity, and generous spirit bring joy and make you the most beloved of sons and the best kind of partner.

Annie, Sing it loud, honey, sing it brave, sing it strong—you are a phenomenal woman in the making and I am so proud and wowed by you.

Maggie Chotas for being the pull to my push, so wise, honest, and real. Thank you for the balance, the friendship, and all the easy laughter.

Acknowledgments

From Maggie, thank you to:

Diannah Champion Ellis, who taught me about power, clarity, and love. Your trust in me has inspired a rooted life with wings. Thank you for showing me how to keep at it.

Marion Arthur Ellis, who inspired in me a zest for research and fostered a love of writing—and still encourages me daily. Thank you for helping shape this book.

Lizzie Ellis-Furlong, whose joie de vivre and amazing skills as a connector have enriched my life many times over.

Harrell Chotas, love of my life, dear friend, sanity saver, and wellspring of present joy. You'll always be right in time with me. Thank you for supporting this project from the very beginning.

Georgia Chotas, daughter, dear soul girl. You have taught me so much about myself, and you bring light and wicked wisdom. Keep on singing your beautiful song!

Nicholas Chotas, curious and nature-loving son. You have taught me how to play (and schooled me in basketball and chess). Keep on keeping on!

And *Betsy Polk,* determined, big-picture-thinking, creative soul sister. We wouldn't have done this without you.

Contributing Partners

Jory Des Jardins, Elisa Camahort Page, and Lisa Stone
  Blogher.com, an online and in-person platform for women

Amy Ray and Emily Salier, singer-songwriters
  The Indigo Girls

Stephanie Allen and Tina Kuna
  Dream Dinners, national franchised meal-preparation company

Ann Patchett and Karen Hayes
  Parnassus Books

Emma McLaughlin and Nicola Kraus, authors
  The Nanny Diaries, The First Affair, and other novels

Cheryl Carolus, Dolly Mokgatle, Thandi Orleyn,
and Wendy Lucas-Bull
  Peotona, South Africa

Gladys Gonzalez and Sandra Gonzalez
  Mundo Hispáno newspaper, Hispanic marketing and consulting (HMC-La Agency)

Deborah Farrington, Laura Sachar, and Jeanne Sullivan
  StarVest Partners, venture-capital firm

Contributing Partners

Lori Joyce and Heather White, reality-show stars and owners
   Cupcakes by Heather and Lori, Canada

Karen McCullah Lutz and Kirsten "Kiwi" Smith, screenwriters *Legally Blonde* and other hit movies

Marian Rees and Anne Hopkins, film producers
   Marian Rees and Associates

Nancy Duff Campbell and Marcia Greenberger
   National Women's Law Center

Linda Kaplan Thaler and Robin Koval
   The Kaplan Thaler Group and authors of *The Power of Nice, The Power of Small,* and *Bang!*

Aziza Hasan and Malka Haya Fenyvesi, mediators
   NewGround: A Muslim-Jewish Partnership for Change

Maria, Lucia, and Angella Ahn, chamber musicians
   Ahn Trio

Amy Gonzalez and Kelly Caldwell
   AK Environmental, environmental, project,
   and construction management

Kelly Alexander and Cynthia Harris, authors
   Hometown Appetites: The Story of Clementine Paddleford, the Forgotten Food Writer Who Chronicled How America Ate

Kella Hatcher and Maryanne Perrin, flexible workplace advocates
   Balancing Professionals

Jennifer Niesslein and Stephanie Wilkinson
   Brain, Child: The Magazine for Thinking Mothers

Bree Shapiro and Molly McDaneld
   Branduin Creative, events and promotions

Isabel Yuriko Stenzel Byrnes and Anabel Mariko Stenzel, authors,
   The Power of Two: A Twin Triumph Over Cystic Fibrosis

Christa Granderson-Reid and Janai Nelson,
   Brownstone Buddies, multicultural dolls

Contributing Partners

Maria, Jennifer, Ursula, Gabrielle, and Charity Burton,
producers, writers, and creators
> Burton Sisters Productions

Zoe Stefanides and Jessica Lee, pharmacists,
> Chapel Hill Compounding

Lori Keith Robinson and Jan Clayton-Pagratis, artists
> Chroma Art Gallery

Kristin B. Leutz and Katie Allan Zobel
> Community Foundation of Western Massachusetts

Amanda Leoni and Amy Cherico
> Down to Earth Aerials

Lynn Ellis and Julie Dokell, event planners
> e-Events

Marirose Steigerwald, Patti Gillenwater, and Kim Foster
> Elinvar, recruitment and executive-coaching firm

Beth Miller and Sarah Troiano, co-founders
> GoodDeeds LLC, life-management company

Jody Thompson and Cali Ressler
> Results-Only Work Environment (ROWE)

Anne Ryan and Christina Lew
> Green-eyed Monster, New Zealand

Stephanie Gordan-Farsht and Ashley Sugalski,
executive-level job-sharers
> Target Corporation

Carin Rosenberg Levine and Julia Lichtman Kepniss Hitched
> Bridal Salon

Teri Johnson and Andrea Adams
> Travelista, travel television program

Frances Gravely and Susan Gravely
> Vietri, handcrafted Italian wares

Contributing Partners

Kendall Allen and Elizabeth Blesser
    Incognito Digital, media-planning company

Meghan Gosk and Anna Millar, job-sharers
    Kenan-Flagler Business School, University of North Carolina at Chapel Hill

Mari Lazar and Kate Tempesta
    Kate Tempesta's Urban Golf Academy

Lauren Parsekian and Molly Thompson
    KIND Campaign, girls' anti-bullying program

Patsy Smith and Lisa Wojnovich, artists
    Litsy Designs

Summer Bicknell and Connie Semans
    LocoPops, Mexican popsicle shops

Perri Kersh and Mary Beth Grealey, home organizers
    NeatFreak

Elizabeth Shea and Kristi Hedges
    SheaHedges Group, public relations and communications for technology companies

Stacey Anderegg, Alison Jones, Betsy Levitas, Marya McNeish, Julie Mooney, Liz Wing, and Julie Woodmansee
a capella singers,
    Stella

Tanya Grubich and Laura Matalon
    The Marketing Group (TMG) (currently Allied Live), theatrical marketing company

Terry Starr and Bradi Nathan
    My Work Butterfly, social and work networking site for women

Wendy Axelrod and Jeannie Coyle
    Talent Savvy Manager, LLC, and authors of *Make Talent Your Business*

Contributing Partners

Jean Hedges and Marilyn Shannon
  Women Power Networking

Dr. Kimberly Gush and Nurse Maria Mekeel
  Village Pediatrics

Valerie Batts and Angela Bryant
  VISIONS, Inc., multicultural consulting

Betsy Brint and Sally Higginson, hosts,
  Walking on Air—Radio Sisters

Robbie Melton, Cynthia Wong, Elizabeth Gray,
and Anne Mathias
  Women in Bio, networking organization
  for female scientists

Julie Smith, Jaime Phillips, and Jessica Reiner
  To the Woods Salon

About the Authors

Amy Stern Photography

Betsy Polk *(left)* is a facilitator, mediator, and board certified coach for The Mulberry Partners who helps people figure out how to build strong partnerships, strengthen collaboration, improve communication, resolve conflict, and achieve goals that stick. In addition to her work with Mulberry, Betsy serves as leadership and organization development consultant for the North Carolina Partnership for Children. She received a bachelor of arts degree from the University of Massachusetts-Amherst and a master of science in organization development from the American University/NTL graduate program in Washington, DC. Betsy is an active volunteer and board member for educationally-focused organizations in Chapel Hill, NC, where she lives with her husband and two lively children.

Maggie Ellis Chotas *(right)* is a facilitator and leadership coach for The Mulberry Partners who started her career as a middle-school teacher and has served as director and consultant for public and independent schools in Philadelphia, New York City, Charlotte, and Durham, NC.

About the Authors

In addition to her work with Mulberry, Maggie serves as senior program manager for NC Ready for Success, a project working to align K–12 and higher education. She is an active community member in Durham, where she lives with her husband and two children. She attained a bachelor of arts degree from Swarthmore College, a master of arts degree from St. John's College in Annapolis, and a master of arts in school administration from the University of North Carolina at Chapel Hill.

About The Mulberry Partners

In 2002, Betsy Polk and Maggie Ellis Chotas found themselves contemplating their next career moves. Both were thinking about additional advanced degrees when they recalled the words of Maggie's mother, "When women think about changing careers, they think they need something else—another degree or more credentials; men just change careers." Motivated by that insight, Betsy and Maggie wove together their complementary skills and formed The Mulberry Partners. Since then, Mulberry has become a leader in strategic planning and leadership development for community-focused organizations, schools, and municipalities. For more information, please visit www.themulberrypartners.com.

Index

Index

Index

Index

Index

Index

Index

Index

Berrett–Koehler
Publishers

Berrett-Koehler is an independent publisher dedicated to an ambitious mission: *Creating a World That Works for All*.

We believe that to truly create a better world, action is needed at all levels—individual, organizational, and societal. At the individual level, our publications help people align their lives with their values and with their aspirations for a better world. At the organizational level, our publications promote progressive leadership and management practices, socially responsible approaches to business, and humane and effective organizations. At the societal level, our publications advance social and economic justice, shared prosperity, sustainability, and new solutions to national and global issues.

A major theme of our publications is "Opening Up New Space." Berrett-Koehler titles challenge conventional thinking, introduce new ideas, and foster positive change. Their common quest is changing the underlying beliefs, mindsets, institutions, and structures that keep generating the same cycles of problems, no matter who our leaders are or what improvement programs we adopt.

We strive to practice what we preach—to operate our publishing company in line with the ideas in our books. At the core of our approach is stewardship, which we define as a deep sense of responsibility to administer the company for the benefit of all of our "stakeholder" groups: authors, customers, employees, investors, service providers, and the communities and environment around us.

We are grateful to the thousands of readers, authors, and other friends of the company who consider themselves to be part of the "BK Community." We hope that you, too, will join us in our mission.

A BK Business Book

This book is part of our BK Business series. BK Business titles pioneer new and progressive leadership and management practices in all types of public, private, and nonprofit organizations. They promote socially responsible approaches to business, innovative organizational change methods, and more humane and effective organizations.

Berrett–Koehler
Publishers

A community dedicated to creating
a world that works for all

Dear Reader,

Thank you for picking up this book and joining our worldwide community of Berrett-Koehler readers. We share ideas that bring positive change into people's lives, organizations, and society.

To welcome you, we'd like to offer you a free e-book. You can pick from among twelve of our bestselling books by entering the promotional code **BKP92E** here: http://www.bkconnection.com/welcome.

When you claim your free e-book, we'll also send you a copy of our e-newsletter, the *BK Communiqué*. Although you're free to unsubscribe, there are many benefits to sticking around. In every issue of our newsletter you'll find

- A free e-book
- Tips from famous authors
- Discounts on spotlight titles
- Hilarious insider publishing news
- A chance to win a prize for answering a riddle

Best of all, our readers tell us, "Your newsletter is the only one I actually read." So claim your gift today, and please stay in touch!

Sincerely,

Charlotte Ashlock
Steward of the BK Website

Questions? Comments? Contact me at bkcommunity@bkpub.com.

MIX
Paper from
responsible sources
FSC® C005010

Certified

Corporation
bcorporation.net